BECOMING GOD
TRANSHUMANISM AND THE QUEST FOR CYBERNETIC IMMORTALITY

TRANSHUMANISM IS an international cultural movement that has as its goal the radical transformation of humanity by the development of technologies that greatly enhance the intellectual, physical and psychological capacities of humans. While a laudable goal—and one that has attracted many supporters from a wide range of perspectives—its roots and fruits lend credence to the objections of Stanford University professor Francis Fukuyama. He ranks the idea as among the most dangerous in history.

Although biologist Julian Huxley is regarded as the founder of the philosophy, basic transhumanist ideas were first articulated by British evolutionist J.B.S. Haldane. Haldane supported the now infamous philosophy of eugenics—the application of genetics to improve humanity—which led to, among other evils, the Nazi Holocaust.

In *Becoming God*, Herbert explores the goals of the transhumanist movement and documents the reasons why it is so dangerous and threatens the values of a free society. Dr. Herbert is a careful and thorough researcher and has written a valuable book that both informs and analyzes this growing movement.

JERRY BERGMAN
Ph.D., professor and author of Hitler and the Nazi Darwinian Worldview

IN THIS telling book, Dr. Herbert shows himself again to be an accomplished scholar and thinker, this time prophetically alerting people to a dangerous and hellish vision of a post-human future percolating among the *intelligentsia*. He has done the public a great service by shedding light on this influential and growing religious movement, but also by leaving us not with foreboding and dread but with the Christian hope.

JOE BOOT
M.A., Ph.D., author, Christian apologist and senior minister,
Westminster Chapel, Toronto, Ontario, Canada

BECOMING GOD

TRANSHUMANISM AND THE QUEST FOR CYBERNETIC IMMORTALITY

DAVID HERBERT

joshua
press

joshua
press

www.joshuapress.com

Published by
Joshua Press Inc., Kitchener, Ontario, Canada
Distributed by
Sola Scriptura Ministries International
www.sola-scriptura.ca

Cover and book design by Janice Van Eck

The publication of this book was made possible by the generous support of
The Ross-Shire Foundation

Library and Archives Canada Cataloguing in Publication

Herbert, David, 1940-, author
     Becoming God : transhumanism and the quest for cybernetic
immortality / David Herbert.

Includes bibliographical references and index.
Issued in print and electronic formats.
ISBN 978-1-894400-58-9 (pbk.).—ISBN 978-1-894400-59-6 (html)

     1. Philosophical anthropology. 2. Theological anthropology.
3. Humanism. 4. Artificial life. 5. Cyborgs. I. Title.

BL256.H47 2014   233   C2014-903492-X
                                         C2014-903493-8

To Lisa Fletcher, Patti Halliday, Matthew Arnold,
Trent Herbert and Chuck Stover

*Over the past two years as fellow interviewers, we have
gathered people's opinions concerning transhumanism;
together we have also logged memories that will not soon
fade away. We were greatly surprised that there was such
a willingness and enthusiasm on the part of the interviewees
to answer the questions related to transhumanism.
By establishing a genuine rapport with these individuals,
we had the privilege of presenting to them the greatest
message pertaining to immortality found only in the death,
burial and resurrection of Jesus Christ.*

CONTENTS

FOREWORD BY JOE BOOT

Ray Kurzweil, a leading transhumanist, has said, "Evolution[ism] is a spiritual process; entities become more god-like, never reaching that ideal but moving in that direction exponentially. So we are going to explode into these very qualities in which God is described."[1] For millennia, people have dreamed of transcending their humanity and becoming more than mere men. The existentialist philosopher Jean Paul Sartre suggested that human beings could in fact be *defined* by their essential desire to be God. This is reminiscent of the biblical text which tells us that the original temptation of the first human pair was that they could "be as God" if they rebelled against the divine commands, and thus realize themselves by asserting their autonomy.[2]

---

1 *Religion & Ethics NewsWeekly* (pbs.org), "Ray Kurzweil: Human Enhancement and Singularity," (July 15, 2011); http://www.youtube.com/watch?v=6XY38r9x5k4&feature=related; accessed April 29, 2014.

2 Genesis 3:5 (ASV).

The ancient Egyptians thought that their Pharaohs were incarnate divinity by virtue of their apparent power and control of natural forces through their magicians and priests. The ancient Greeks held that people could graduate from being heroic men to the status of gods, living between the worlds. And the Roman republic worshipped the Caesars and believed the emperor joined the pantheon of gods after death; the Roman senate regularly made such declarations.

This basic, even innate, desire to redefine created reality and become more than a creature, a limited and mortal human being, has not gone away. Eastern thought (which has enjoyed huge popularity in the West in recent decades), in Hinduism and Buddhism respectively, holds that what we think of as the self is ultimately absorbed into the "one" or the divine, whether this is described as "being" or "non-being." The Eastern gods or their physical avatars are manifestations of the one essence. The German philosopher G.W.F. Hegel held that the state (elite men as the apex of rationality) was god walking the earth as a kind of incarnation of world spirit, with all men being essentially scattered bits of god-consciousness awaiting reunification into the one, for full "god" consciousness to emerge.

Adolf Hitler and the Nazis believed in the evolutionary and scientific creation of a race of super men, a religious vision of Arian demi-gods. And Karl Marx thought that "material man" as the new god could *recreate* himself through work and scientific industry, ushering in a utopian age without any need for the God of Scripture.

Today, a growing syncretistic movement of transhumanists among the *intelligentsia*, borrowing elements from all of the above, has taken the next logical step in the development of a humanistic, neo-pagan anthropology and social vision based on the ancient idea of evolutionism. These scientists, business leaders, technologists, futurists, politicians and artists place a messianic hope in the ideal of a *post-human* world, holding that the key to humanity's future lies in realizing godhood (omniscience, immortality, etc.) by the merging of man with his technology. That is, what was once thought possible by ascending a scale of being inherent in the universe through heroism, or mystical incantation, man now will accomplish by the *control* of evolutionism through his own technological work and his *merging* with what he has created.

As David Herbert shows us in this volume, these evocative ideas are not the views of a handful of eccentric computer geeks or would-be Jedi warriors glued to their screens in their parents' basement, but represent a growing movement of intellectuals and practitioners in diverse fields who hold these convictions with religious fervour, supported by financial and political reach. The transhumanists believe that their view of man and the future is not merely a social manifesto, but a religion, capable of uniting people and pointing forward to a godlike destiny. For these technocratic priests, having experienced a merging with technology, the human body and mind transformed, the future will lead to venturing out from the earth to explore limitless space. This next evolutionary step will mean the universe is finally awake since, in the new post-human cyborg, god is born.

For most of us ordinary mortals, talk of cyborgs, cryonics, nanobots, digital immortality and an endless exploration of outer space, belongs to the entertaining world of *Star Trek* and like science fiction creations. However, as Dr. Herbert concisely and insightfully explains, these advocates of transhumanism believe that within a generation (inside of forty years) information technology will have become so advanced that biological thought and physicality will merge with technology, transcending the limits of the human species—the difference between the human and the machine, steadily disappearing. Nanobots will be injected into the bloodstream, eventually making people immortal cyborgs connected with a singularity or super-computer in the "cloud."

At first blush this just sounds like an amusing dream, but Herbert convincingly demonstrates the logic of this developing thought, beginning with Enlightenment thinkers through to today's transhumanists, and reveals the seriousness of their proposals. Once you have jettisoned the God of Scripture as the

Enlightenment did, evolutionism becomes the key player on the stage of history in human thought. Rather than being subject to its blind whims, as in nineteenth- and early-twentieth-century evolutionary ideas, man must now seek to control his own evolution and realize his own idea of himself as god—the universe thus becoming self-conscious.

With a lightness of touch and the precision of a historian, Herbert thus skillfully shows us what undergirds the thought of transhumanists in the history of philosophy and carefully describes the informational and technological developments that actuate their hopes for the future. For example, forty or fifty years ago, our super-computers in major universities like MIT took up the best part of a building in terms of required space, and cost millions of dollars. Today, the computer in our cell phones is a million times smaller, a million times less expensive and a thousand times more powerful, than those monster computers. With such a scale and speed of technological advance, and in the wake of the invention of the Internet, the transhumanists believe a post-human reality is near, to the point that one day we will be able to download our consciousness into a machine and live forever in a digital heaven—presuming no-one pulls out our plug!

Herbert then reveals how this is little more than a technological and dystopian Tower of Babel and that the true answer to man's longing for life and immortality has been brought to light only through Jesus Christ and his resurrection. In Christ, God the Son became flesh, a real human being, and affirmed the glory and value of our humanity. By his bodily resurrection, he pointed to the immortal and corporeal future of those in Jesus Christ. We will never be God, but we can participate in Christ's perfect humanity as those made in God's likeness, and so share his holiness. In him, death shall be swallowed up by life and the mortal shall be clothed in immortality.[3]

In this telling book, Dr. Herbert shows himself again to be an accomplished scholar and thinker, this time prophetically alerting

---

3   See 1 Corinthians 15:54.

people to a dangerous and hellish vision of a post-human future percolating among the *intelligentsia*. He has done the public a great service by shedding light on this influential and growing religious movement, but also by leaving us not with foreboding and dread but with the Christian hope.

JOE BOOT

M.A., Ph.D., author, Christian apologist and senior minister, Westminster Chapel, Toronto, Ontario, Canada

ACKNOWLEDGEMENTS

I n 2011, Calvin Smith of Creation Ministries International wrote: "Transhumanism—mankind's next step forward? Will mankind evolve into a perfect being?"[1] After having read the article, my son Trent suggested that I should consider transhumanism as a topic for research—hence, the birth of this book. Calvin and Trent made another significant contribution in that they both reviewed the manuscript.

I would like to express my appreciation to my wife, Irene, for her conscientious proofreading.

As an author, I greatly treasure the assistance of the peer reviewers mentioned below: David Barker, Th.D., vice president of academic and student affairs, Heritage Theological Seminary, Cambridge, Ontario, Canada; Nikola Danaylov, M.A., podcast host of *Singularity 1 on 1*, Toronto, Ontario, Canada; Andrew McLeod,

---

1 Calvin Smith, "Transhumanism—Mankind's Next Step Forward? Will Mankind Evolve into a Perfect Being?" Creation Ministries International (February 3, 2011); http://creation.com/transhumanism-mankinds-next-step-forward; accessed April 29, 2014.

B.A., M.Div., historian, London, Ontario, Canada; Natasha Vita-More, M.Sc., Ph.D., adjunct professor, University of Advancing Technology, Tempe, Arizona, USA; Brent Waters, Ph.D., the Jerre and Mary Joy Stead Professor of Christian Social Ethics, Garrett-Evangelical Theological Seminary, Evanston, Illinois, USA; Harvey Zhu, Ph.D., visiting Chinese scholar, Ivey Business School, University of Western Ontario, London, Ontario, Canada.

To the five mentioned in the dedication, who braved all types of weather to assist me in conducting interviews, I am deeply indebted.

Finally, I want to thank Joe Boot for writing the foreword to my book in which he eloquently captured its message.

OO

INTRODUCTION

On January 16, 1874, Charles Darwin (1809–1882) was asked to attend a séance. It was arranged by his older brother, Erasmus (1804–1881), who had invited his favourite American medium Charles Williams. Gathered at Erasmus Darwin's London home were such prominent Victorians as his cousins Francis Galton (1822–1911) and Hensleigh Wedgwood (1803–1891), novelist and journalist Mary Ann Evans (1819–1880) known by her pen name George Eliot, and also a number of Charles' children.[1]

Charles, per usual, became tired and withdrew to lie down; he later reported that he missed witnessing "the chairs, a flute, a bell, and candlestick, and fiery points jump about in my brother's dining room in a manner that astounded everyone, and took

---

1 For a detailed account of the séance, see Roger Luckhurst, *The Invention of Telepathy* (Oxford: Oxford University Press, 2002), 37–39.

away all their breaths."[2] In spite of these manifestations, in a letter two weeks later to Thomas Huxley (1825–1895), often called "Darwin's bulldog" for his aggressive defence of evolutionism, Charles stated unequivocally that "to his mind an enormous weight of evidence would be requisite to make one believe in anything beyond mere *trickery*…the more I thought of all that I had heard happened at Queen Ann St., the more convinced I was it was all *imposture* [deception]."[3]

Darwin, the father of evolutionism, was indeed convinced that all forms of spiritualism were fraudulent, but his brother's circle of friends possessed a different mindset. Contrary to the premises of evolutionism in which the universe was viewed as purposeless and that humanity had a bestial past, these eminent Victorians rebelled against such a philosophy of life. "Darwin forced them to ask why their lives should not end like those of other animals, in nothingness. If this was so, how could human existence have meaning?"[4]

To these intellectuals, spiritualism offered the much-needed solace which was so lacking in Darwinism. They had rejected all traditional forms of religion. But "still, the human need for a meaning in life that religion once satisfied could not be denied, and fueled the faith that scientific investigation would show that the human story continues after death."[5]

The desire for immortality, witnessed in the lives of these nineteenth-century British luminaries, has continually plagued human history from Sumer—our most ancient known civilization— to the present. In his most recent book, *Immortality: The Quest to Live Forever and How it Drives Civilization*, Stephen Cave has

---

2   Charles Darwin, *The Life and Letters of Charles Darwin*. ed. Francis Darwin, 2 vols. (New York: Basic Books, 1959), 2:364.

3   Darwin, *The Life and Letters of Charles Darwin*, 2:365. Author's italics.

4   John Gray, *The Immortalization Commission: Science and the Strange Quest to Cheat Death* (Toronto: Doubleday Canada, 2011), 21.

5   John Gray, "John Gray on Humanity's Quest for Immortality," *The Guardian* (Saturday, January 8, 2011); http://www.guardian.co.uk/books/2011/jan/08/john-gray-immortality; accessed April 29, 2014.

Charles Darwin (1809–1882) is considered the father of evolutionism. His influential book, *On the Origin of Species by the Preservation of Favoured Races in the Struggle for Life*, was first published in 1859.

identified four means by which civilizations (or individuals) throughout history have approached the pursuit of immortality. They are:

1. Scientific progress[6] (Emperor Qin[7] and transhumanism).
2. Resurrection (Christianity and Islam).
3. Immortal soul (Hinduism and Buddhism).
4. Lasting legacy (Alexander the Great and Charles Darwin).

The purpose of this book is to demonstrate how both humanism and Darwinism facilitated the rise of Dr. Cave's first or "scientific" option—transhumanism. For twenty-first-century futurists, this ideology has caused them to envision a distinct possibility that humanity could merge with technology and become post-human.

The historical roots of transhumanism can be traced to the Enlightenment era, known as the Age of Reason (1688–1789). Even though the French Revolution cast a dark shadow over the Enlightenment ideals, the supremacy of reason persisted and made its presence felt in nineteenth-century England. One of the most significant events of the Victorian era was the emergence of Darwinism—the first religious pillar of transhumanism.

In the United States, during the twentieth century, humanism[8]—the second pillar—captivated the imagination of many North Americans. In 1933, *Humanist Manifesto I*, a reasoned approach to religion, was formulated. The theme was: "Religious humanism: Being religious without God." Forty years later, *Humanist*

---

6 Stephen Cave subtitles this as "Staying Alive."

7 Qin Shi Huang (259–210 B.C.), China's first Emperor, was advised by his court alchemists to ingest a daily elixir which was guaranteed to give him the longevity that he so desired. Unfortunately, the concoction, it is surmised, was laced with either mercury, lead or arsenic, or, worst still, all three. Needless to say, his death was slow and excruciatingly painful.

8 Humanism is a religious commitment that centres solely on human reason and ingenuity. Humanists believe that they "can discover no divine purpose or providence for the human species. While there is much that we do not know, humans are responsible for what we are or will become. No deity will save us; we must save ourselves" [*Humanist Manifestos I and II*, ed. Paul Kurtz (Buffalo: Prometheus, 1973), 16].

Manifesto II set the stage for the emergence of secular humanism; its basic premise was: "Being good without God and religion."

By the 1990s, with secular humanism and Darwinism firmly embedded within the Western world, the theological climate was ideal for the rise of transhumanism. The vision that humanity could attain immortality—hence "becoming God"—was for the first time a reality within the foreseeable future. This radical transformation would be facilitated by breathtaking advances in computer and medical technologies.

Four transhumanists—three American and one British—have revealed their desire to gain cybernetic immortality. The most prominent is American futurist, Ray Kurzweil (b. 1948). He has set "the date for the singularity—representing a profound and disruptive transformation in human capacity as 2045."[9]

Recognized internationally, the World Transhumanist Association has a present membership estimated to be around 8,000—primarily within academia.[10] It's philosophy statement, according to its popular *Humanity+* magazine, includes:

Transhumanism is a class of philosophies of life that seek the continuation and acceleration of the evolution of intelligent life beyond its current human form and human limitations by means of science and technology, guided by life-promoting principles and values.[11]

Dr. Cave's second option for gaining immortality was resurrection. The promise of a resurrected body, which will be similar to

9 Ray Kurzweil, *The Singularity Is Near: When Humans Transcend Biology* (New York: Viking, 2005), 136.

10 Michael Anissimov, "World Transhumanist Association Exceeds 5,000 Members," *Accelerating Future* (May 26, 2008); http://www.acceleratingfuture.com/michael/blog/2008/05/world-transhumanist-association-exceeds-5000-members/; accessed April 30, 2014. The article also stated that recruitment had been averaging about 500 per year—thus the current estimate of membership at around 8,000.

11 Citing Max More (1990), "Philosophy," *Humanity+* (2012); http://humanityplus.org/philosophy/philosophy-2/; accessed June 2, 2014.

the one possessed by the Lord Jesus Christ, is one of the hall-marks of the Christian faith. The Bible categorically states to all followers of Jesus Christ, "if Christ has not been raised, your faith is worthless."[12]

In order to gauge the general public's reaction to transhuman-ism, I developed a three-part questionnaire. Those to whom this book is dedicated have assisted me in interviewing individuals throughout London, Ontario, Canada. The results are shown in the appendix.

A CHRISTIAN BIAS

Early in the semester of a senior history class on modern European history, I began a unit on the recognition of bias within all histor-ical sources. I made the categorical assertion that it was impossi-ble for any individual to write a historical account without reveal-ing his or her bias.

A student, raised in the Middle East, challenged me. Even though he had personally experienced the ravages that the Israeli army had inflicted upon his nation, he was convinced that he had the ability to write a short but unbiased account of the conflict between his country and Israel. The next morning before class, this student candidly admitted that I was absolutely correct. As much as he had tried, he was unable to divorce himself from his deep-rooted animosity toward the Israeli forces.

In honour of that particular student and all the other students that I had the privilege of teaching the importance of detecting bias, I will, as I have done in all my books, specify mine. Such a declaration is extremely vital as I am not only looking at the historical roots of transhumanism and its impact, but I will be analyzing its philosophical foundations in light of those of Christianity. I am a committed Christian who believes that the

---

12 1 Corinthians 15:17. All scriptural references will be from the New American Stan-dard Bible (NASB). The Greek word for worthless is *mataia*, meaning "devoid of truth, a lie." See A.T. Robertson, *Word Pictures in the New Testament: Epistles of Paul*, Vol. 4 (Nash-ville: Broadman, 1931), 190.

Bible is the authoritative Word of God. It, and only it, possesses the absolute truths concerning life and immortality.

THE SPIRIT OF THE ENLIGHTENMENT

In 1798, Napoleon Bonaparte (1769–1821) invaded Egypt. Imbued with the spirit of the Enlightenment, this conqueror took not only his troops but a corps of French savants, which "included astronomers, civil engineers, draftsmen, linguists, Orientalists, painters, poets, and musicians."[13] One year later, it was these same scholars who recognized the importance of the Rosetta Stone, which had been unearthed while constructing fortifications against an impending British attack.

The Rosetta Stone, containing three inscriptions—Egyptian hieroglyphics, demotic and *koiné* Greek—initiated a twenty-three-year search which resulted in the eventual deciphering of hieroglyphics. In September 1822, Jean-François Champollion (1790–1832) accomplished the incredible feat.

The Egyptian *cartouche*, an oval shape (originally a circle) that encircled the name of a pharaoh, became a critical tool employed by Champollion in uncovering a language that had been untranslatable for nearly two centuries. "To write the name of the pharaoh inside a *cartouche* was both a religious and magical act to protect the pharaoh and ensure he would live for ever."[14]

The importance of the pharaoh's *cartouche* in maintaining his immortality is an ideal *segue* into our discussion on the Enlightenment. It was the Enlightenment's elevation of human reason that set an eighteenth-century foundation for the eventual emergence of transhumanism—hopefully to be the twenty-first-century vehicle to attain everlasting life.

---

13 Lesley and Roy Adkins, *The Keys of Egypt: The Obsession to Decipher Egyptian Hieroglyphs* (New York: HarperCollins, 2000), 10.

14 Adkins, *The Keys of Egypt*, 194.

| 1700 | 1800 | 1900 | 2000 |

01

THE ENLIGHTENMENT
The foundation of reason

HISTORICAL SETTING

"Sapere aude! 'Have courage to use your own reason!'— that is the motto of enlightenment" was written by Immanuel Kant (1724–1804) in his essay, *What is Enlightenment?*[1] By focusing upon human reason or rationality, the illustrious German philosopher succinctly encapsulated the central theme of this pivotal period of history. Historian Roy Porter has correctly noted that its influence has been perpetuated until this present day. Thus, he makes this very penetrating observation: "As the Enlightenment's children, we should try to fathom our parents."[2]

There has been little consensus among historians as to the appropriate time frame for the Enlightenment, also called the

---

1   Isaac Kramnick, ed., *The Portable Enlightenment Reader* (New York: Penguin, 1995), 1. *Sapere* is a present infinitive of *sapio*, meaning "to dare," while *aude* is a present imperative of *audeo*, meaning "to know."

2   Roy Porter, *The Creation of the Modern World: The Untold Story of the British Enlightenment* (New York: W.W. Norton, 2000), xii.

Age of Reason. Peter Gay, a noted Professor Emeritus of History at Yale University, has suggested that the one-hundred-year Enlightenment era began with the Glorious Revolution (1688) in England[3] and came to a close at the beginning of the French Revolution (1789).[4]

During this period, France became the intellectual centre of Europe, with French replacing Latin as the *lingua franca* or universal language. An English landowner advised his son that, by being able to speak French, he would not only be viewed as sophisticated but he could be understood everywhere. Trends in fashion took their lead from Paris. "Everyone who could afford it employed a French chef."[5]

Nevertheless, it was an international movement. Its impact could be seen in Germany, Russia, Scotland and even in the United States. In the latter, the Declaration of Independence and its framers were greatly influenced by Enlightenment ideals. Not everyone, including the well-known evangelical scholar, Jonathan Edwards (1703–1758), whose most famous sermon was: "Sinners in the Hands of an Angry God" (1741), was enthralled with this new worldview. In his book, *The History of the Work of Redemption*, he wrote against the Enlightenment's rejection of the Christian interpretation of history. He correctly foretold that this denial of an omniscient God's total involvement in the redemptive plan for humanity would lead to "the de-Christianization and the secularization of history."[6]

---

3 With the accession to the British throne by William III of Holland and his wife, Mary, Protestantism and the British parliamentary system had been firmly established by a bloodless revolution.

4 Peter Gay, "The Little Flock of Philosophes" in *The Enlightenment: Critical Concepts in Historical Studies*, ed. Ryan Patrick Hanley and Darrin McMahon, 5 vol. (London: Routledge, 2010), 1:112.

5 N. Hampton, "The Enlightenment" in *A Dictionary of Eighteenth-Century World History*, ed. Jeremy Black and Roy Porter (Oxford: Blackwell, 1994), 115.

6 Avihu Zakai, *Jonathan Edwards's Philosophy of History: The Reenchantment of the World in the Age of Enlightenment* (Princeton: Princeton University Press, 2003), 39.

COFFEE HOUSES AND SALONS

The emergence of coffee houses—an Enlightenment phenomenon—provided individuals with the opportunity to exchange ideas about current events and the pressing issues of life. In London, England, alone, there were 2,000 establishments.[7] They were termed "penny universities" as they welcomed all individuals regardless of their station in life for a mere entry fee of a penny. In some coffee houses, this British egalitarianism, was extended even to women.

The *salons*—a uniquely French venue—differed greatly from the British coffee houses. They were gathering places in the homes of prominent French women. These hostesses, known as *salonnières*, not only selected who could attend, but they chose and supervised the topics to be discussed. Steven Kale in his book, *French Salons*, made this salient observation:

> A *salonnière* treated her *salon* as her own creation and took responsibility for what happened there—those entering her *salon* did so expecting to follow her rules. Conversational enjoyment and efficacy required the enforcement of certain rules of decorum and demanded the avoidance of topics that might be too thorny to ensure congeniality or too arcane to allow everyone to participate.[8]

The *salons* came to symbolize the heart of the Enlightenment fervour. It was an ideal platform for the *philosophes*, recognized as leading intellectuals or men of letters, to exercise reasoned judgements and opinions concerning the affairs of the day. More often than not, they were radical, especially against the autocratic and repressive actions of the Roman Catholic church or the French government. Such criticism came with a cost. The *philosophes*

---

7 Francis Sharpstene, "Women of French Salons and English Coffee Houses, 18th Century Enlightenment" (2010); http://www.youtube.com/ watch?v=SbRGIFIBcQk; accessed April 30, 2014.

8 Steven Kale, *French Salons: High Society and Political Sociability from the Old Regime to the Revolution of 1848* (Baltimore: Johns Hopkins University Press, 2004), 23.

"could fall foul of the authorities and suffer persecution. They sometimes needed to flee their homes for safe havens in more liberal countries."[9]

One of the most renowned and influential salons was hosted by Madame Geoffrin (1699–1777). It was a badge of distinction to be invited to her Paris home. Every Monday afternoon, artists graced her tables to enjoy a sumptuous dinner after which they were engaged in lively discussions and debates. On Wednesday afternoons, the *philosophes* were welcomed and experienced the same. Not sparing her time, energy and financial resources, the efforts of this *salonnière* were rewarded as "princes or ambassadors, church dignitaries, celebrated statesmen, authors and artists" were more than eager to be invited to her salon.[10] Even though the queen of the Parisian *salonnières* was born a *bourgeois* or commoner, she was courted by the monarchs of Europe.[11] For a five-year period, Madame Geoffrin corresponded with Catherine the Great of Russia (1729–1796).

THE RISE OF DEISM

Deism—a rational theism—attracted a considerable following, especially within the French *intelligentsia*. Ironically, this new religion has its roots in England. Edward Herbert of Cherbury (1583–1648), a British philosopher, has come to be recognized as the originator of English deism. His writings, written in Latin, contended that divine providence had implanted within humans common principles of worship. In his *De veritate (On truth)* written in 1629, he said these innate notions "constitute an important part of the image of God in man. And their truth is attested by universal consent."[12] Five cardinal principles in Baron Herbert's deism were:

9 Graeme Smith, *The Short History of Secularism* (New York: Tauris, 2008), 140.

10 Janet Aldis, *Madame Geoffrin: Her Salon and Her Times, 1750–1777* (New York: G.P. Putnam's sons, 1905), xi.

11 E.B. Hall, *The Women of the Salons* (Freeport: Books for Libraries Press, 1926; reprint 1969), 41.

12 Sarah Hutton, "Lord Herbert of Cherbury and the Cambridge Platonists" in *British Philosophy and the Age of Enlightenment*, ed. Stuart Brown (London: Routledge, 1996), 21.

Edward Herbert, 1st Baron Herbert of Cherbury (1583–1648) is considered the father of English deism.

1. There exists only one supreme God.
2. Mankind's duty is to revere this God.
3. Adoring worship of God must be practiced in conjunction with applied principles of morality.
4. If man repents his sins and improves his behaviour, God will forgive.
5. Good works are rewarded both before and after death.[13]

Deism, as practiced in France, differed from its British counterpart in one highly significant way. The Bible no longer played a central role in their worship of God. The French *philosophes,* who naturally gravitated to deism, outrightly dismissed the Bible as being totally incompatible with human reason. These men of letters discarded "several core features of church Christianity like revelation, miracles, means of grace, the Incarnation, the divine inspiration of the Scriptures and a divinely ordained ecclesiastical hierarchy."[14]

The French *philosophes*, as those in other countries, overwhelmingly supported Baron Herbert's first proposition. This Supreme Being or First Cause who brought the universe into existence *ex nihilo* (out of nothing), wound it up like a clock and let it run for an eternity. As an absentee landlord, this Creator-God abandoned his creation to the physical laws that he established. Since God was remote and not involved in the affairs of the world, the *philosophes* viewed the movement of history as *Historia Humana*—an Enlightenment approach which "emphasized human freedom and autonomy in the shaping of history."[15]

THREE VIEWS ON GOD, DEATH AND IMMORTALITY OF THE SOUL

During the eighteenth-century Enlightenment period, "death was at the centre of life as graveyards were at the centre of the

---

13 Barbara Schwarz Wachal, "Deism," in *Gale Encyclopedia of US History* (2012); http://www.answers.com/topic/deism; accessed April 30, 2014.

14 "Introduction," in *British Philosophy and the Age of Enlightenment*, 8.

15 Zakai, *Jonathan Edwards's Philosophy of History*, 10.

village."[16] Statistics from that time reveal that per 1,000 births, only 200 would reach the age of 50 and only 100 the age of 70.[17] Thus, the average lifespan would be around thirty-five years of age.[18] Death was so commonplace that a funeral procession caused little notice. With the shadow of death ever looming, religion, with its hope and solace in the life to come, became foremost in the thoughts of the French populace.

Not having an objective authority, such as the Bible, and depending solely on human subjectivity, the *philosophes*, as one would expect, established diametrical views regarding God, death and the immortality of the soul. Let's examine the three main views.

VOLTAIRE: A LASTING LEGACY

François-Marie Arouet de Voltaire (1694–1778) wholeheartedly subscribed to the first principle of classical deism. A prolific writer, Voltaire covered every literary genre "whether it be prose, poetry, plays or history; he wrote 2,000 books or pamphlets and sent or received 20,000 letters—a phenomenal literary output."[19] Viewing God as not only aloof and austere, Voltaire wondered why this Supreme Being would "concern himself with the puny affairs of mankind; we are rats on a ship bound for an unknown destination, we are mice lost in a castle constructed by the divine architect for his own mysterious purposes."[20]

This indifferent God, Voltaire reasoned, cared little even if an individual in utter desperation committed suicide. In reality, "death

---

16 John McManners, *Death and the Enlightenment: Changing Attitudes to Death Among Christians and Unbelievers in Eighteenth-Century France* (Oxford: Oxford University Press, 1981), 5.

17 McManners, *Death and the Enlightenment*, 5. Every year, 25 per cent of all newborns would die. "Being born was a hazardous business for both mother and child" (McManners, *Death and the Enlightenment*, 8).

18 McManners, *Death and the Enlightenment*, 92. Not surprisingly, young boys were conscripted into the French army at the age of 15. Living conditions in the barracks, being cramped and squalid, took their toll on these young recruits.

19 David Herbert, *The Faces of Origins: A Historical Survey of the Underlying Assumptions from the Early Church to the Twenty-First Century*, rev. ed. (Kitchener: Joshua Press, 2012), 88.

20 McManners, *Death and the Enlightenment*, 173.

was an eternal sleep."[21] According to Voltaire, there was no tangible evidence to substantiate the soul's existence or its immortality. Furthermore, immortality, a fanciful myth, was used to placate the credulous masses. Accordingly, hell, too, was a human construct to deter people's evil inclinations. From Voltaire's perspective, hell as a deterrent has never worked, since perversity has always persisted—thus, hell must be deemed an absurdity!

Voltaire was aware that in the depth of every individual's heart was a yearning for immortality. This illustrious *philosophe* maintained that immortality can be attained, not by spiritual means, but rather through a lasting legacy of being remembered by one's family and friends. For some, like Voltaire, their names would survive for generations to come.

JEAN-JACQUES ROUSSEAU: IMMORTAL SOUL

Jean-Jacques Rousseau (1712–1778) readily accepted the five propositions of classical deism. This famous social and educational philosopher viewed God as one who was the essence of goodness and compassion. This Deity, "in creating us, had assumed obligations towards us, to authenticate the hopes and longings implanted in our hearts."[22] Death could not bring finality to human existence.

Rousseau envisioned that this Supreme Deity, being consistent with his benevolent nature, would reward both the unjust and just. But, to the unjust, he would provide a suitable punishment which would not be eternal damnation. The concept of hell was utterly repulsive to a loving God. Universalism—the belief that all will be in God's presence—was firmly held by Rousseau. In the end, every "soul will spring up, vigorous and jubilant"[23] and achieve peace and fulfillment forever.

An American, Lysander Spooner (1808–1887) fully supported Rousseau's views concerning the immortality of the soul. In an 1834 essay titled, "The Deist's Immortality," this schoolteacher

---

21 McManners, *Death and the Enlightenment*, 161.

22 McManners, *Death and the Enlightenment*, 173–174 .

23 McManners, *Death and the Enlightenment*, 174.

François-Marie Arouet de Voltaire (1694–1778), a deist and one of the best-known *philosophes*, believed in the inevitable progress of humankind and that death was an eternal sleep.

Jean-Jacques Rousseau (1712–1778), a deist, held to universalism, a belief that all immortal souls would eventually be in God's presence. He could not conceive of the existence of hell.

turned lawyer portrayed heaven in even more irenic terms where everyone will forever experience intellectual and moral progress. "Our natures therefore are capable of being eternally carried nearer and nearer to perfection solely by the power of causes, which we see to be already in operation."[24]

JULIEN OFFRAY DE LA METTRIE: CESSATION OF EXISTENCE

Julien Offray de la Mettrie (1709–1751) was considered the *bête noire* of his day. A surgeon by training, he lambasted the Paris Academy of Medicine for their lack of providing instruction in basic anatomy and chemistry. He likewise was highly critical of his fellow physicians for their medical incompetence. The medical community on a regular basis added undue suffering and misery to their patients' conditions.

From 1745 to 1751, this outspoken doctor turned his attention to philosophical matters. He penned ten anonymous works in which he forthrightly articulated his materialistic viewpoints. His first book, *The Natural History of the Soul* (1745), stated that, as a physician, he had never seen the soul and, in reality, it and God never existed. Death, a natural occurrence, ended human existence. This book caused such a hue and cry that this *médecin-philosophe* was forced to flee from Paris to Leiden, Holland.

Three years later, while still living in Leiden, he wrote *L'homme machine (Machine Man)* which would undoubtedly become his most famous work. The second last paragraph succinctly summarizes the book:

> Let us then conclude that man is a machine and that there is in the whole universe only one diversely modified substance.... I would have disdained a guide that I consider to be so uncertain if my senses, carrying the torch, so to speak, had not encouraged me *to follow reason* by lighting

---

24 Lysander Spooner, "The Deist's Immortality," (2010 edition); http://oll.libertyfund. org/?option=com_staticxt&staticfile=show.php%3Ftitle=2290&chapter=216955&layout=html&Itemid=27; accessed May 1, 2014.

its path. Experience thus spoke to me in *reason's favor* and
so I applied them together.[25]

Elie Luzac, La Mettrie's French Protestant publisher, who did
not share his client's atheistic views, made the book available to
the public in 1748. The vitriolic attacks against *Machine Man* were
predictable. In order to allay such intense public anger, a church
council of Leiden was convened to address the matter. They
demanded that Luzac destroy all existing copies of this crassly
materialistic book; he immediately complied. But he could not
resist surreptitiously circulating "enough copies of *L'homme
machine* to gratify the increasing curiosity of the reading public."[26]
Luzac then fled from Leiden.

At the same time, La Mettrie made a speedy exit to Berlin, the
capital of Prussia. Here, Frederick II (1712–1786), a widely recognized supporter of Enlightenment ideals, not only extended
refuge to this notorious author, but appointed him to be his personal physician.

To add insult to injury, La Mettrie continued to publish books
from Prussia, but he turned his attention to the development of
human moral and ethical behaviour. His humanistic medical perspective led him to the conclusion that, when peering into nature,
one must conclude that humans were not different from animals.
"Just as virtue and vice were not terms assigned to animals, neither
could they be used to describe the actions of humans in the state
of nature."[27] Thus, for humans, these notions of morality were
learned within the context of society.

Consequently, society, through its moral conditioning, must
assume some of the blame for individuals' deviant behaviour.
Education, this scholar reasoned, could provide some means of

---

25 Julien Offray de la Mettrie, *Machine Man and Other Writings*, ed. Ann Thomson,
(Cambridge: Cambridge University Press, 1996), 39. Author's italics.

26 Aram Vartanian, ed., *La Mettrie's L'homme Machine: A Study in the Origins of an Idea*
(Princeton: Princeton University Press, 1960), 7.

27 Kathleen Wellman, *La Mettrie: Medicine, Philosophy and Enlightenment* (Durham:
Duke University Press, 1992), 216.

Julien Offray de la Mettrie (1709–1751), a surgeon/philosopher, denied the existence of God and believed that death ended human existence. He authored the influential *L'homme Machine (Machine Man)* in 1748.

rectifying anti-social misconduct. But La Mettrie soon realized that he was in an ethical quagmire: How do you develop a moral consciousness within an offender but at the same time provide the necessary protection demanded by the public? As a moral philosopher, he could offer no solution.

La Mettrie's biographer, Dr. Kathleen Wellman, noted that La Mettrie was a man ahead of his time. By 1770, many of his materialistic beliefs became accepted.[28] A case in point was Denis Diderot (1713–1784), the editor of the illustrious *Encyclopédie*. He had been a committed deist but later in his life became an atheist who essentially held the same beliefs as La Mettrie but suffered no reprisals.

THE FRENCH REVOLUTION

During the early years of the Revolution, both England and the United States applauded the overthrow of the oppressive French monarchy and the Roman Catholic church. But such approval turned to horror with the inception of the Reign of Terror (1793–1794).

The emergence of the supremacy of reason over revelation became very prominent in the Enlightenment's view of theology. But its impact was not in France but rather in Germany. The rational approach to biblical studies, which would become known as "Higher Biblical Criticism," took root in the German universities. Without a doubt, this element of Enlightenment ideology would branch out into all facets of the Western world and leave an enduring impact in the coming centuries.

---

28 Wellman, *La Mettrie*, 240.

02

THE VICTORIAN ERA
The triumph of reason

HISTORICAL SETTING

Queen Victoria (1819–1901) became monarch of the British Empire on June 20, 1837. During her nearly sixty-four-year reign—the longest in British history—England would be "transformed into an industrial democracy."[1] In 1851, the Great Exhibition, the brainchild of Victoria's German husband, Prince Albert (1819–1861), came "to symbolize the industrial, military and economic superiority of Great Britain."[2] Some six million visitors from all over the world came to enjoy the five-month exhibition. The newly constructed railway system provided them with a fast and efficient means of transportation to the site at Hyde Park in London.

But, on their arrival, it was the building, "a huge iron goliath with over a million feet of glass," that showcased the grandeur of

---

1   Sally Mitchell, *Daily Life in Victorian England*, 2nd ed. (Westport: Greenwood, 2009), xiv.

2   1851 News, "The Great Exhibition"; http://www.uk1851census.com/news.htm; accessed May 1, 2014.

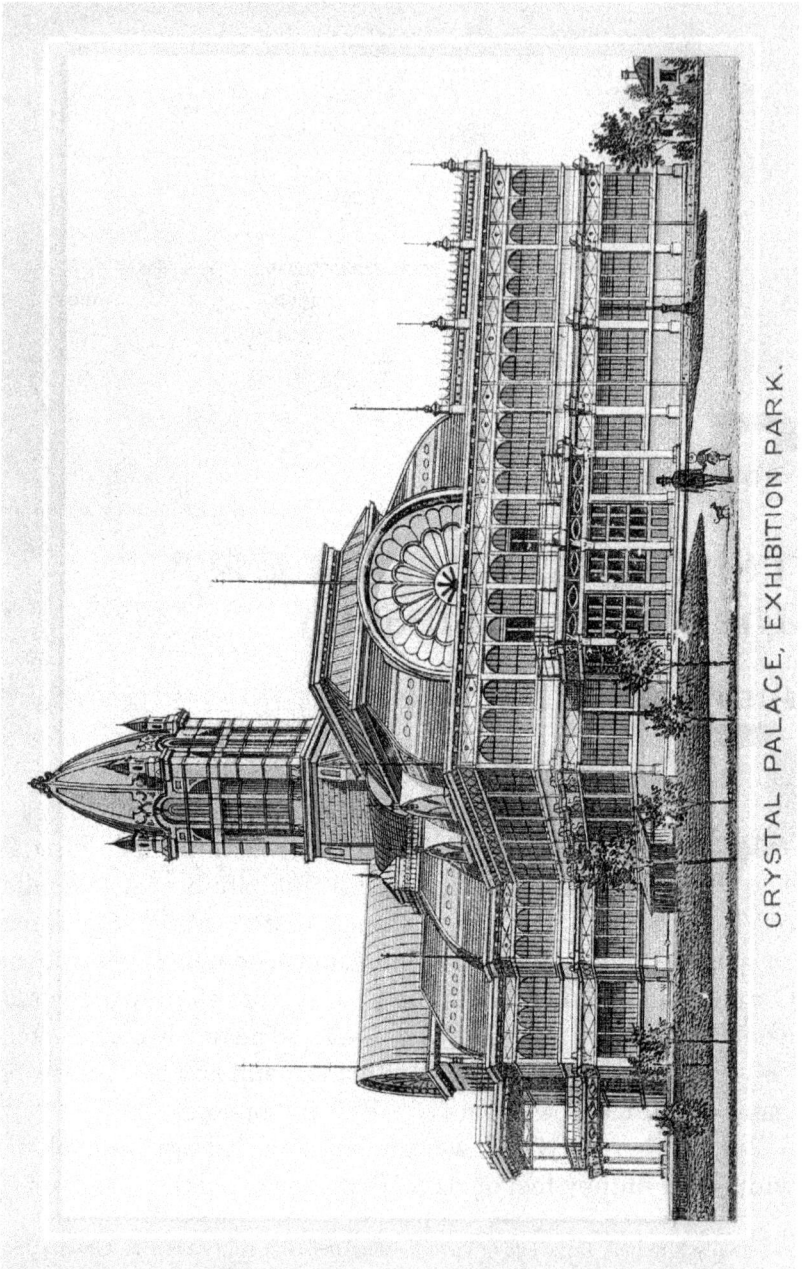

CRYSTAL PALACE, EXHIBITION PARK.

The Crystal Palace at Britain's Great Exhibition (1851) was designed by Joseph Paxton. It housed 13,000 exhibits from all over the world.

the exhibition.[3] Designed by Joseph Paxton (1803–1865), The Crystal Palace housed 13,000 exhibits from every corner of the globe.[4] No one, leaving this impressive edifice and its surrounding parkland, with a series of magnificent fountains and statues, had the slightest doubt that Great Britain was the leader of the Industrial Revolution.

Industrialization has always been linked to the idea of progress, "clearly the most prized legacy of the Enlightenment."[5] Being placed on a high pedestal and heralded as the panacea of enduring and limitless knowledge and prosperity, industrialization also brought forth a darker side. Its factories, located in crowded and squalid cities, subjected its employees to intolerable working conditions, especially young children; they were required to work long hours and received much lower wages than adults.

In the midst of this flurry of technological advancement, the religious landscape of Britain underwent drastic changes. At the beginning of the nineteenth century, a wave of evangelicalism swept the country. But, during the latter half of the century, liberal Christianity, influenced by German biblical criticism, emerged. Its commitment to secularism set the religious course for England; this humanistic outlook continues to make an impact in England today.

THE EVANGELICAL ERA

Prior to the nineteenth century, religious activity was set within the bounds of the state and the church. But the outdoor preaching of revivalists, such as John Wesley (1703–1791) and George Whitefield (1714–1770), challenged the religious status quo. They "laid stress on faith in the context of the individual as a 'free moral

---

3 1851 News, "The Great Exhibition"; http://www.uk1851census.com/news.htm; accessed May 1, 2014.

4 1851 News, "The Great Exhibition"; http://www.uk1851census.com/news.htm; accessed May 1, 2014.

5 Brent Waters, *From Human to Posthuman: Christian Theology and Technology in a Postmodern World* (Hampshire: Ashgate, 2006), 12.

agent.'"[6] This emphasis on a personal relationship with God through "the new birth" became the motivation for evangelism.

The advent of the Industrial Revolution brought large masses of people into the cities, especially in places like Manchester and Birmingham. These factory workers who were experiencing the drudgery of long hours of labour, the overcrowded living conditions and the spiritual hopelessness were ripe for the message of hope provided by the gospel of Jesus Christ.

This spiritual awakening can be attributed to the "Protestant evangelicals of Nonconformity who were critical, exerting an influence well beyond their numbers."[7] Their effectiveness can be explained in part by noting the Christian organizations that they established. This period has been termed, "The Age of the Great Religious Societies."[8] Two that should receive honourable mention would be the Religious Tract Society and the Young Men's Christian Association (YMCA).

It became very apparent early in this evangelical movement that religious tracts or flyers could easily communicate the gospel message to large numbers of people. The tract was essentially a short sermon; it might focus on a specific social problem, but it would direct the reader to scriptural passages through which an individual could be freed from the burden of personal guilt, find forgiveness and receive eternal life through the redeeming work of Jesus Christ. In 1799, the Religious Tract Society was formed in London. In its first two years of operation, it distributed over a million tracts.[9] Fifty years later, the London City Mission distributed 9,771 Bibles and 2,970,527 tracts in one year.[10]

In 1837, while apprenticing for a drapery business, George Williams (1821–1905) committed his life to Jesus Christ. He was

---

6 Callum G. Brown, *The Death of Christian Britain: Understanding Secularisation, 1800-2000* (London: Routledge, 2001), 36.

7 Brown, *The Death of Christian Britain*, 43.

8 H.C. Cross, *One Hundred Years of Service with Youth: The Story of the Montreal YMCA* (Montreal: Southham, 1951), 3.

9 Brown, *The Death of Christian Britain*, 49.

10 Brown, *The Death of Christian Britain*, 46.

Queen Victoria (1819–1901) pictured in 1875. During her nearly sixty-four-year reign, England was swept up into the Industrial Revolution.

appalled by the spiritual condition of the young men who were migrating to London to find jobs and were continually confronted with evil choices. In 1844, he and twelve other men formed the first YMCA.

The mandate of the YMCA was to provide a spiritual refuge for young men through weekly Bible studies and prayer. In a matter of a few years, the movement had spread across London, and, in 1851, it gained international recognition during the Great Exhibition. "No less than 320,000 copies of readable Christian literature were distributed, each pamphlet containing full information about the YMCA."[11] In that same year, the YMCA was established in Montreal, Canada, and Boston, USA. The period between 1870 and 1930 was its high point spiritually. The YMCA program combined both biblical training and sports activities.

Within the middle and lower classes of Britain, Christianity made considerable inroads. The Bible had become an honoured book that was believed and obeyed. At the mid-point of the nineteenth century, Britain would be considered a Christian country. But a spiritual tidal wave, emanating from Germany, was already sweeping across the English channel; its force was directed against the Bible—the foundation of Christianity.

GERMAN BIBLICAL CRITICISM EMBRACED IN GREAT BRITAIN

The Enlightenment's influence on biblical studies in Germany differed greatly from that in France. Rather than attacking the Roman Catholic church, the German theologians raised questions and sought answers concerning the historicity and accuracy of the Scriptures; the Bible was placed under the scrutiny of human reason. The end result was that German scholars began to attack the very foundation of Christianity—the Bible itself. With human reason at the helm, humanism, emanating from German institutes of higher learning, took a devastating toll on Western Christianity.

---

11 Cross, *One Hundred Years of Service with Youth*, 13.

Christian Gottlob Heyne (1729–1812), the director of the library at the University of Göttingen and a prolific author, publicized the concept that mythological thought was "the universal mode of thinking and expression in humanity's infancy."[12] But it was Johann Gottfried Eichhorn (1752–1827), a distinguished professor at both the universities of Jena and Göttingen, who introduced Heyne's mythic interpretation into biblical studies, specifically the Old Testament.

DAVID STRAUSS' *LIFE OF JESUS CRITICALLY EXAMINED*

The application of this mythic approach to the New Testament was accomplished through the work of David Friedrich Strauss (1808–1874). He received his philosophical training at the University of Tübingen. In 1832, he returned to his *alma mater* to teach philosophy. During his short tenure, he taught Eduard Zeller (1814–1908) who, in a letter to his father, wrote:

My favorite lectures are those given by Strauss. Never have I found such a clarity and dialectical dexterity combined with such ardor and warm conviction as in this man.... This fact and the great reputation which he had here already explain why his lectures up till now have been so well attended that he has had to seek a larger auditorium.[13]

Such glowing praise from Zeller spoke volumes regarding Strauss' teaching ability. A decade later, Dr. Zeller, founder of the influential periodical, *Theologische Jahrbücher*, published material that was very supportive of his mentor's theological stance.

In the autumn of 1833, Strauss terminated his classroom duties and focused his undivided attention on his monumental book,

---

12 Edwina Lawler, *David Friedrich Strauss and His Critics: The Life of Jesus Debate in Early Nineteenth-Century German Journals* (New York: Peter Lang, 1986), 23.

13 Horton Harris, *The Tübingen School: A Historical and Theological Investigation of the School of F.C. Baur* (Leicester: Apollos, 1990), 61–62.

The Life of Jesus Critically Examined. Adopting his own mythic mode of interpretation,[14] he argued that the four Gospels were "a collection of legendary stories based on the knowledge of a Galilean teacher and leader who lived a pure life."[15] Following Jesus' death, Christian writers claimed him to be the Messiah whose righteous life was marked by miraculous deeds and an indomitable passion to fulfill God's will.

In his discussion concerning Jesus' virgin birth, this New Testament critic stated that both the supernatural explanation must be discounted "in order to escape the ridicule of our contemporaries" and, similarly, the naturalistic one as it "leads to conclusions not only extravagant, but revolting."[16] Consequently, the only remaining option would be the mythic approach.

Dr. Strauss wrote: "In the world of mythology many great men had extraordinary births and were sons of the gods."[17] Placing Jesus' birth alongside Hercules of Greece and Romulus of Rome, Strauss successfully destroyed any historical foundation for the biblical account. Throughout his colossal treatise, some 1,600 pages in the German version, this twenty-five-year-old theologian systematically shredded the historical fabric from the Gospel writings. The "biblical" remnants "must, consequently, be demythologized, desupernaturalized and demiracleized."[18] Strauss was convinced that the New Testament writers were not fraudulent but, since they became so committed to supernaturalism, they had become misguided.

---

14 See an excellent article by Marcus Borg, "David Friedrich Strauss: Miracle and Myth," Weststar Institute (1991); http://www.westarinstitute.org/resources/the-fourth-r/david-friedrich-strauss/; accessed May 1, 2014. Dr. Borg clearly shows that Strauss disagreed with both the rationalists (deists) who denied the miracles ever occurred and the supernaturalists who maintained that they did. Consequently, he formulated his own mythic methodology.

15 Victor Shea and William Whitla, eds., *Essays and Reviews: The 1860 Text and Its Reading* (Charlottesville: University of Virginia Press, 2000), 58.

16 David Friedrich Strauss, *The Life of Jesus Critically Examined*, ed. Peter C. Hodgson and trans. George Eliot (Philadelphia: Fortress, 1972), 140.

17 Strauss, *The Life of Jesus Critically Examined*, 140.

18 Horton Harris, *David Strauss and His Theology* (Cambridge: Cambridge University Press, 1973), 283.

David Friedrich Strauss (1808–1874) was the first to apply "German Higher Criticism" to the New Testament, calling the four Gospels "a collection of legendary stories," in his deeply polarizing book, *The Life of Jesus Critically Examined.*

The Life of Jesus Critically Examined not only rocked the theological establishment but it changed the image of Tübingen University "from a center of orthodoxy into a center of heresy."[19] This perception persisted throughout the nineteenth century. A book of such notoriety caused extreme polarization. In a letter to his brother on July 1, 1835, Eduard Zeller, expressing the sentiments of his theological peers, wrote: "It is really an excellent book, very scholarly to be sure, but pleasingly written, like a novel, and deadly hostile to all orthodox Christianity."[20]

In the meantime, at the other end of the spectrum, Strauss' heretical treatise caused this young philosopher to be dismissed from his teaching position at the University of Tübingen. David Strauss' argument "that 'myth' is not simply to be equated with 'falsehood'" had become accepted.[21]

In 1844, Mary Ann Evans began the translation of *The Life of Jesus Critically Examined* from German into English. Translating six pages a day, she completed this tome in two years. This was her first major work. Later, she would become a brilliant editor at which time she adopted the pseudonym, George Eliot. Under this *nom de plume*, she would become one of England's renowned novelists.

The English version of *The Life of Jesus Critically Examined* had an enormous impact on British society, especially in the upper class. Personally, Mary Ann Evans came to accept David Strauss' theology which caused her to jettison biblical Christianity and develop a very sympathetic attitude toward unitarianism.

THE GROWTH OF RATIONALISM: UNITARIANISM AND DEISM

During the first half of the nineteenth-century in Great Britain, amid the flurry of evangelicalism, unitarianism and deism also flourished. Under the leadership of Joseph Priestley (1733–1804),

---

19 Harris, *The Tübingen School*, 2.
20 Harris, *The Tübingen School*, 63.
21 Borg, "David Friedrich Strauss: Miracle and Myth."

the discoverer of oxygen, unitarianism, more correctly called "biblical" unitarianism, had a high regard for the Bible as a source of personal inspiration and morality. But, since Unitarians maintain the oneness of God, they reject the traditional trinitarian view of God as being contrary to human reason. Priestley taught that "Jesus Christ was a human leader to be followed not worshipped."[22]

In 1851, this denomination had 229 congregations across Britain with a membership of some 30,000 people.[23] This religion, based on the rational, attracted a number of high-profile people, namely: Josiah Wedgwood (1730–1795), the founder of the fine pottery industry in Staffordshire and the maternal grandfather of Charles Darwin; John Stuart Mill (1806–1873), philosopher and political economist; and Florence Nightingale (1820–1910), the founder of modern nursing.

Deism differed greatly from unitarianism in that it was a *personal* belief system rather than being an organized *denomination*. The two-volumed *Age of Reason*, authored by Thomas Paine (1737–1809), clearly set forth the basic tenets of deism. It stated:

> Deism teaches us, without the possibility of being deceived, all that is necessary or proper to be known. The creation is the Bible of the Deist. He there reads in the handwriting of the Creator himself, the certainty of His existence and the immutability of His power; and all other Bibles and Testaments are to him forgeries.... The only religion that has not been invented, and has in it every evidence of divine originality, is pure and simple Deism.[24]

Paine's *Age of Reason* was a vitriolic attack on Christianity. The British government deemed it to be not only seditious but blasphemous. Any publisher who dared to print this dastardly book

---

22 "Unitarian Society," Spartacus Educational; http://www.spartacus.schoolnet.co.uk/PRunitarian.htm; accessed May 1, 2014.

23 "Unitarian Society."

24 Thomas Paine, *The Complete Writings of Thomas Paine*, ed. Philip S. Foner, 2 vol. (New York: Citadel Press, 1945), 1:599–600.

would face a fine or imprisonment or both. In 1819, Richard Carlile (1790–1843), "a contrary and hotheaded printer-publisher with a taste for confrontation,"[25] contravened the law by publishing *Age of Reason*. Arrested and found guilty of blasphemy, he spent nine years in prison. Between 1818 and 1822, Carlile claimed that he "sent into circulation 20,000 copies of the *Age of Reason*."[26]

Deists, not having a place to worship on Sunday, felt very comfortable attending a Unitarian church. Deist Charles Lyell (1797–1875), author of the three-volumed *Principles of Geology* (1830–1833), and his wife were very active in the Unitarian church in London.

ESSAYS AND REVIEWS (1860)

The publication of *Essays and Reviews* on March 21, 1860, announced to the general public that rationalism had been readily accepted in—of all places—the Anglican Church. Six of the authors were Anglican clergy, while the seventh was a lawyer and an amateur geologist. These seven essayists, known as the "Seven Against Christ,"[27] wanted the Bible to be interpreted in light of the advances of German biblical criticism, Darwinian evolutionism and the newest methods of historical investigation.[28] These scholars asserted that the Bible must be subjected to the same rules of textual analysis as any other book. Reason, not biblical doctrine, should form the basis for a sound and relevant interpretation.

Even though *Essays and Reviews* was printed four months after Charles Darwin's *On the Origin of Species*, it caused a much greater furore. The British people were shocked that the Anglican church leadership would have the audacity to make known publicly their denial of the inspiration of the Bible, miracles and the historicity of the Scriptures. Nevertheless, in nine years and in its thirteenth edition, the book's sales had reached 24,250 copies. By means of comparison, it was not until 1876—some

---

25 Joss Marsh, *Word Crimes: Blasphemy, Culture and Literature in Nineteenth-Century England* (Chicago: University of Chicago Press, 1998), 60.

26 Marsh, *Word Crimes*, 71.

27 Ieuan Ellis, *Seven Against Christ: A Study of 'Essays and Reviews'* (Leiden: Brill, 1980).

28 Shea and Whitla, eds., *Essays and Reviews*, 9.

seventeen years after *Origin* was first published—that Darwin's book had sold 17,000 copies.[29]

The outcry against *Essays and Reviews* came not only from the British press. In 1861, the editor of the *Christian Guardian*, a weekly Toronto Methodist newspaper, regretted that the Church of England had sunk to such depths of apostasy. "The religious world," he wrote, "was hardly prepared for the revelation that 'the Church' harboured and supported in her most important posts men who were avowed unbelievers in revealed religion."[30]

But three decades later, the initial objections were totally forgotten or ignored. Frederick Temple (1821–1902), author of the first article in *Essays and Reviews*, was appointed Archbishop of Canterbury, the highest office in the Anglican Church. Indeed, humanism had been quietly and unceremoniously ushered into the most preeminent seat of religious power within Britain!

VIEWS ON IMMORTALITY: CHARLES AND EMMA DARWIN

In 1839, Charles Darwin and Emma Wedgwood Darwin (1808–1896), his first cousin, were married at St. Peter's Anglican Church in Maer, Staffordshire, England. Even at their marriage, their individual beliefs about the afterlife were well formulated. Emma, representing an overwhelming majority of Victorians, believed in heaven. On the other hand, Charles was a deist; he differed from classical deism as he did not believe that there were any types of rewards or punishments after a person's death.[31]

Charles and Emma made their first home in London. Here Charles, who began to systematize his nearly 5,500 specimens collected on his five-year voyage on the HMS *Beagle*,[32] was able to

---

29 Shea and Whitla, eds., *Essays and Reviews*, 25.

30 Editorial, "Infidelity in the Anglican Church: the *Essays and Reviews*," *Christian Guardian* (April 24, 1861): 66.

31 See the author's *Charles Darwin's Religious Views*, rev. ed. (Kitchener: Joshua Press, 2009), 59–62.

32 Rebecca Stott, *Darwin and the Barnacle: The Story of One Tiny Creature and History's Most Spectacular Scientific Breakthrough* (London: Faber and Faber, 2003), 65.

collaborate with leading scholars in geology and zoology. On Sundays, they attended the Unitarian Chapel with Hensleigh, Emma's brother, and his wife, Fanny.[33]

Choosing to worship at the Unitarian Chapel was totally consistent with the Wedgwood religious tradition. As a family, they were "Unitarian by conviction, Anglican by practice."[34] Henrietta, their daughter, recalled after her mother's death: "She went to church regularly and took the Sacrament. She read the Bible with us and taught us a simple Unitarian Creed, though we were baptized in the Church of England."[35] Without a doubt, Emma was a typical "biblical" unitarian.

Attending the Anglican church was to maintain a social status within the community; but her true convictions embraced unitarianism with its denial of the Trinity and the deity of Jesus Christ. For Emma, Jesus' manner of life was a model that everyone should follow. Not believing in the inherent sinfulness of humanity, she saw no merit in his vicarious atonement. Instead, Emma believed that everyone who believed in God, and lived a life of caring and helping others, would receive eternal life at death.

The essential element of Emma Darwin's faith was the solace of reuniting with loved ones after death. In 1832, her sister Fanny (1806–1832), just two years older, died. The two siblings had been inseparable; they were known as "Miss Salt and Miss Pepper."[36] Darwinian biographer, Janet Browne conveyed Emma's innermost feelings: "More than anything else, she needed to believe that there was a heaven, and that, if she was good and kind, she would go there."[37] Nineteen years later in 1851, her eldest

---

33 Randal Keynes, *Annie's Box: Charles Darwin, His Daughter and Human Evolution* (New York: Riverhead, 2002), 10.

34 James F. Moore, *The Darwin Legend* (Grand Rapids: Baker, 1994), 36.

35 *Emma Darwin: A Century of Family Letters, 1792–1896*, ed. Henrietta Litchfield, 2 vol. (London: John Murray, 1915), 2:173.

36 Deborah Heiligman, *Charles and Emma: The Darwin's Leap of Faith* (New York: Holt, 2009), 37.

37 Janet Browne, *Charles Darwin: Voyaging* (New York: Knopf, 1995), 396.

Emma Wedgwood Darwin (1808–1896), like most Victorians, believed in heaven. She saw it as the place where she would be reunited with loved ones.

daughter, Annie, died at the age of ten. She told Henrietta (Annie's younger sister by two years) that "Annie was safe in Heaven."[38]

A year or so before their marriage, Charles had rejected his commitment to "biblical" unitarianism and had become a deist. Throughout their forty-three years of living together, the daunting thought that Charles' disbelief in God would cause their separation after death continually haunted Emma. She wrote to him shortly after their marriage warning Charles of the consequences of disregarding the Bible, gently reminding him: "Every thing that concerns you concerns me and I should be most unhappy if I thought we did not belong to each other forever."[39]

Deism seemed to Charles to be the only rational option. He was undoubtedly influenced by Charles Lyell who had been his geological mentor and was also a deist. In a letter written to Lyell in 1865, Charles related his fear that the universe and life itself would end in oblivion. The death of a mutual friend and paleontologist Hugh Falconer (1808–1865) prompted the father of evolutionism to write:

> I had not heard of poor Falconer's suffering before receiving your note. The thought has quite haunted me since… everyone has his own pet horror and this slow progress or even *personal annihilation* sinks in my mind into insignificance compared with the idea, or I presume certainty, of the sun some day cooling and we all freezing. *To think of the progress of millions of years, with every continent swarming with good and enlightened men all ending in this.*[40]

On a personal level, Charles' deism was also shaped by his commitment to materialism. He believed that one's present life was the totality of existence. In his *The Descent of Man, and*

---

38 Charles Darwin, *The Correspondence of Charles Darwin*, ed. Frederick Burkhardt and Sydney Smith, 19 vol. (Cambridge: Cambridge University Press, 1985–2012), 5:543. Hereafter, it will be cited as Darwin, *Correspondence*.

39 Darwin, *Correspondence*, 2:172.

40 Darwin, *Correspondence*, 13:56. Author's italics.

Selection in Relation to Sex (1871), he declared that humans were nothing more than animals; thus, not possessing any spirit, at death they ceased to be. With such an outlook, it was inevitable that he despaired so deeply at Annie's passing. She was gone forever, never to be seen again!

But in spite of this pessimistic viewpoint, he still sought for immortality. Charles found the answer in his last book, *The Formation of Vegetable Mould, through the Action of Worms, with Observations as to Their Habits* (1881)—earthworms! British psychotherapist Adam Phillips (b. 1954) in his book, *Darwin's Worms*, wrote: "It is as though the earth is reborn again and again passing through the bodies of worms. Darwin had replaced a creation myth with a secular maintenance myth."[41] In a similar vein, American psychiatrist, Ralph Colp (1924–2008) stated that Darwin believed that "his remains will move through the bodies of worms and perform some useful function."[42]

At the coronation of Queen Victoria in 1837, a biblical supernatural worldview prevailed. Some sixty-five years later at her death in 1901, a naturalistic worldview, committed to German biblical criticism in tandem with Darwinian evolutionism, had captivated the hearts and minds of people in the Western world. Charles Darwin's *On the Origin of Species* was translated first into German (1860) and then French (1862). These languages were "crucial, as these could be read by learned elites throughout Europe and the rest of the world."[43]

---

41 Adam Phillips, *Darwin's Worms: On Life Stories and Death Stories* (London: Faber & Faber, 1999), 58.

42 R. Colp, "The Evolution of Charles Darwin's Thoughts About Death," *Journal of Thanatology* 3 (1957): 201.

43 James A. Secord, "Global Darwin," in *Darwin*, ed. William Brown and Andrew C. Fabian (Cambridge: Cambridge University Press, 2010), 50. On the next page, Secord lists thirty countries and the dates in which *Origin* was translated.

03

RELIGIOUS HUMANISM
Being religious without God

HISTORICAL SETTING

We must inevitably win this war for we are biologically right; we are the fittest to live, and hence nature is with us. That group which can dominate other groups is the chosen of evolution. It should struggle with other groups and it should win over them and dominate them *for the sake of the evolutionary advance* of the human race.[1]

Such audacious claims were uttered in 1915 by a German infantry captain to Vernon Kellogg (1867–1937). Since the United States was a neutral country during the first three years of the Great War (1914–1918), Dr. Kellogg was granted a leave of absence from his teaching duties at Stanford University to provide humanitarian relief for civilians in Belgium

---

1   Vernon Lyman Kellogg, *Germany in the War and After* (New York: Macmillan, 1919), 99. Author's italics.

and northern France. Having done graduate work in entomology at the University of Leipzig, this American scholar was fluent in German and often invited to dine with high-ranking officers of the German High Command. He published these conversations in *Headquarters Nights*.[2]

Professor Kellogg was an ardent Darwinian who penned "a constant stream of books, reviews, addresses and research papers."[3] *Darwinism Today* (1907) was his most popular work. But Kellogg was still aghast that this German captain, a zoologist at a prominent university prior to the war, would maintain that warfare, and especially a German victory, would be a boon for the advancement of the human race.

Secretly, Kellogg abandoned his previously held pacifism and began using his influence to encourage the United States to enter the war in order to end such reprehensible ideals. He wrote:

> I was convinced, however, that this war, once begun, must be fought to the finish or decision—a finish that will determine whether or not Germany's point of view is to rule the world. And this conviction, thus gained, meant the conversion of a pacificist, to an ardent supporter, not of War, but of this war.[4]

"To drink at the fountain of German scholarship"[5] was the dream of many aspiring intellectuals during the nineteenth century and into the first two decades of the twentieth century. It has been estimated that 9,000 young American men attended German

---

2   Vernon Lyman Kellogg, *Headquarters Nights: A Record of Conversations and Experiences at the Headquarters of the German Army in France and Belgium* (Boston: The Atlantic Monthly Press, 1917).

3   C.C. McClung, *Biographical Memoir of Vernon Lyman Kellogg* (Washington: National Academy of Science, 1938), 248.

4   Kellogg, *Headquarters Nights*, 23.

5   Jurgen Herbst, *The German Historical School in American Scholarship. A study in the Transfer of Culture* (Ithaca: Cornell University Press, 1965), 2.

universities between 1820 and 1920, of whom fifty per cent chose the University of Berlin.[6]

In light of such statistics, noted evangelist and college professor, Thomas Theodore Martin (1862–1939), speaking on behalf of many Americans, stated: "We send our young men to the German universities, and, when they come back, saturated with Evolution[ism], we make them Presidents and head-professors of our colleges and great universities."[7] Three northern universities—Chicago, Michigan and Columbia—were noted for their connection with German rationalism.

A collision course between this university-based humanism and a commonly held biblical supernaturalism occurred in the classroom in Dayton, Tennessee, in 1925, over the teaching of evolutionism. The conflict centred around John Scopes (1900–1970) who supposedly taught evolutionism and thus violated the Tennessee Anti-Evolution Act of March 21, 1925.[8] His trial provided a legal battlefield for two renowned lawyers, William Jennings Bryan (1860–1925) and Clarence Darrow (1857–1938). Both of these men were known nationally: the former, a three-time Democratic presidential candidate, and the latter, a prominent criminal lawyer.

Bryan, an evangelical, defended the state law, while Darrow, a humanist, opposed it. On the surface, the trial was definitely a first-rate media event. It attracted both national and international attention as "the rural courtroom was wired with the latest technology, using every possible means to broadcast the proceedings to the world."[9] But below the surface, the two worldviews, biblical supernaturalism and humanism, were involved in a

---

6 Herbst, *The German Historical School in American Scholarship*, 16.

7 Adam Laats, *Fundamentalism and Education in the Scopes Era: God, Darwin, and the Roots of America's Culture Wars* (New York: Palgrave McMillan, 2010), 4.

8 In his autobiography, written three decades later, Scopes admitted that he did not teach the topic of evolutionism. See John Scopes and James Presley, *Center of the Storm: Memoirs of John T. Scopes* (New York: Holt, Rinehart and Winston, 1967), 30.

9 Mano Singham, *God vs. Darwin: The War between Evolution and Creationism in the Classroom* (Lenham: Rowman & Littlefield, 2009), 30. The technology included radio, movie newsreels, telegraph and telephone.

vitriolic spiritual struggle. In 1925 and a few years beyond, the
creationists won the skirmish but, as the remainder of the book
will show, the evolutionists won the hearts of the masses.

THE FOUNDER OF RELIGIOUS HUMANISM

Roy Wood Sellars (1880–1973) was born in Seaforth, Ontario,
Canada. When he was four years of age, his family moved to
Michigan where his father set up his medical practice. After completing his basic education, he enrolled, in 1899, at the University
of Michigan, known as the "Athens of the West."[10]

As a philosophy student, he studied under a faculty thoroughly
committed to German rationalism. Besides being instructed in
Darwinian evolutionism, he would come to believe that the pro-
ponents of higher biblical criticism had "dissected the Bible in a
quest to prove that it was nothing more than an edifying collection of Semitic myths."[11]

W. Preston Warren, Sellars' biographer, noted that the young
Sellars was a diligent university student; "on graduation his class
voted him one of the two most scholarly of its members."[12] After
completing his doctorate at the University of Michigan in 1908,
Dr. Sellars travelled to Europe to continue his post-doctoral studies in Germany and France during 1909 and 1910.

Throughout his life, Professor Sellars was a prolific writer; during the period between 1916 and 1928 he wrote six books. Following
the ravages of World War I, this university scholar sensed that the
North American public was poised to abandon the traditional religions and was ready to accept a new belief system—religious humanism. Consequently, he penned *The Next Step in Religion: An
Essay Toward the Coming Renaissance* (1918) and *Religion Coming of
Age* (1928); they were applauded by Unitarians and humanists
alike for their "attractive, homely style of writing."[13]

---

10 Jay Martin, *The Education of John Dewey: A Biography* (New York: Columbia
University Press, 2002), 85.

11 Laats, *Fundamentalism and Education in the Scopes Era*, 13.

12 W. Preston Warren, *Roy Wood Sellars* (Boston: Twayne, 1975), 20.

13 Bill Cooke, *A Wealth of Insights: Humanist Thought Since the Enlightenment* (Amherst:

His first basic premise in his pursuit of religious humanism was that "religion was an inescapable aspect of life."[14] Similar to biological evolutionism, Sellars believed religion had developed over millennia of time until it reached Christianity—"the high-water mark of theology."[15] The ethical demands of Christianity should be heeded by all. But the dawning of a new religious age could only be attained by a thorough purging of a belief in God. Humanism, a religion devoid of any revelation, was based on this resolve:

> Let man stand on his own feet and trust his own powers. The universe is not unfriendly; rather is it the natural scene of his birth and achievements. It is something within which to work in a human way, bravely, creatively, gently, wisely.... Here we have man and religion coming of age.[16]

In 1933, Raymond Bragg (1902–1979), an associate editor of the *New Humanist*, first published in 1927, was confident that many within the Unitarian community wanted a clear declaration of what it meant to be a religious humanist. Sellars, a pioneer and published authority on religious humanism, was approached to submit a draft proposal of the main tenets of this belief system. Based on his extensive research, including his lecture notes at the University of Michigan, Professor Sellars submitted the first draft under the title, *Humanist Manifesto I*—a title he coined.

THE HUMANIST MANIFESTO I (1933)

After numerous revisions, the *Humanist Manifesto I* was published in the May/June 1933 issue of the *New Humanist*. Its preamble affirmed the vital role that religion has always played within human existence. But since "man's larger understanding of the

---

Prometheus, 2011), 89.

14 Roy Wood Sellars, *Religion Coming of Age* (New York: Macmillan, 1928), 143.

15 Roy Wood Sellars, *The Next Step in Religion: An Essay Toward the Coming Renaissance* (New York: Macmillan, 1918), 59.

16 Sellars, *Religion Coming of Age*, 156.

universe, his scientific achievements and his deeper appreciation of brotherhood,"[17] had greatly increased, a new religion was needed. This new religion must focus solely on human needs and responsibilities.

The *Manifesto* was well received by the press; the Associated Press, *Time* and the *Christian Century* broadcasted the document across the nation.[18] Within the humanist camp, there was criticism. Harlow Shapley (1885–1972), an astronomer and director of the Harvard Observatory, articulated the most common reason why many refused to sign the *Manifesto* when he wrote:

> Personally, I feel that I should keep clear knowing my ignorance, from any movement to which the word religion can be attached openly. I try to be a scientist. Science is chiefly a matter of the intelligence; religion is chiefly a matter of the emotions.[19]

Fifteen articles constituted the *Humanist Manifesto I*. As a statement of faith, it began with its cosmological position. The universe, as stated in the first article, was "self-existing and not created."[20] Humanity, addressed in the second, was viewed as being identified with all of nature but emerged "as the result of a continuous process."[21] It should be noted that no direct reference to Darwinian evolutionism was mentioned.

The twelfth article was highly significant in that religious humanism would provide "joy in living" and was designed "to foster the creative in man and to encourage achievements that

---

17 Paul Kurtz, ed., *Humanist Manifesto 1 and II* (Buffalo: Prometheus Books, 1973), 8.

18 "Chapter 17: Twenty Years Later: Symposium I and II" in Edwin H. Wilson, *The Genesis of a Humanist Manifesto* (Amherst: The Humanist Press, 1995); http://infidels.org/library/modern/edwin_wilson/manifesto/ch17.html; accessed May 2, 2014.

19 "Chapter 7: Critiques from Humanists Who Did Not Sign: Harlow Shapley" in Wilson, *The Genesis of a Humanist Manifesto*.

20 Kurtz, ed., *Humanist Manifesto 1 and II*, 8.

21 Kurtz, ed., *Humanist Manifesto 1 and II*, 8.

add to the satisfaction of life."[22] The essence of the authors' intent was captured in the concluding paragraph: "Though we consider the religious forms and ideas of our fathers no longer adequate, the quest for the good life is still the central task for mankind."[23]

There were thirty-four signatories. Two distinctive features of these initial signers were that the majority were Unitarians and many were in some way connected to three northern universities—Chicago, Michigan and Columbia. Secondly, a sign of the 1920s would be that women were excluded and all those who endorsed the document were men.

Undoubtedly, the most renowned signatory was John Dewey (1859–1952)—acclaimed as "one of the greatest twentieth-century philosophers."[24] Interestingly enough, he had taught at all of the aforementioned universities. His prolific writings concerning educational philosophy had been translated into many languages.

The name of Clarence Darrow, the defense lawyer of the famous Scopes Trial (1925), and outspoken humanist, did not appear. The implementers of the *Humanist Manifesto I* very much wanted his endorsement but, apparently, he failed to respond to their invitation.

Edwin Wilson (1898–1993) who has written the most comprehensive history of the *Manifesto* concluded his book with this insightful statement: "Upon rereading *Humanist Manifesto I*, its naiveté is clear. Equally clear, however, are the ways in which the document has transcended the past six decades."[25]

ROY WOOD SELLARS' VIEWS ON IMMORTALITY

The 1920s, often called the Roaring Twenties, were marked with prosperity, new ideas and personal freedom. Consequently,

---

22 Kurtz, ed., *Humanist Manifesto 1 and II*, 10.

23 Kurtz, ed., *Humanist Manifesto 1 and II*, 10.

24 Alan Ryan, *John Dewey and the High Tide of American Liberalism* (New York: Norton, 1995), 47.

25 "Chapter 18: The Manifesto's Long-Term Impact: A Final Note" in Wilson, *The Genesis of a Humanist Manifesto*.

Dr. Sellars observed that North American society was "entering upon a period of religious deflation,"[26] particularly in its relationship to Christianity. Over many years of studying religious history, Sellars concluded that the architects of Christianity were responsible for *creating* the concept of immortality.

In his book, *Religion Coming of Age*, Dr. Sellars then posed this thought-provoking question: "Can religion dispense with the belief in immortality?"[27] His reply was a definite, "Yes!" But, as a professional philosopher, he felt that, before such an action could be attempted, a pertinent question must be broached: Why do people desire to extend their life beyond the grave? He listed four reasons:

1. The dislike for annihilation.
2. The desire to meet again those we have loved.
3. The hope for a dramatic display of justice.
4. The craving for a persistence of human values.[28]

Professor Sellars briefly discussed each possibility, but he discounted each one with this rationale:

> I see no reason why a calm, old age with a long life to look back upon should not be prepared for death as a *natural and inevitable event*. ... People may learn to grow old charmingly to meet death cheerfully as *the final withdrawal* of the forces of life. After all, is not death the price we pay for life?[29]

Furthermore, his monistic approach to human life dictated that every individual was solely physical—devoid of a spirit. Such a position was totally consistent with his evolutionary perspective of life in which humans were nothing more than mere animals.

---

26 Sellars, *Religion Coming of Age*, 184.
27 Sellars, *Religion Coming of Age*, 200.
28 Sellars, *Religion Coming of Age*, 197.
29 Sellars, *Religion Coming of Age*, 198. Author's italics.

In 1932, when Sellars was asked to produce the first draft of the *Humanist Manifesto I*, he was able to express his well-formulated view on immortality in the eighth article:

> Religious humanism considers the complete realization of human personality to be the end of man's life and seeks its development and fulfillment in the here and now.[30]

---

30 Kurtz, ed., *Humanist Manifesto 1 and II*, 9.

04

SECULAR HUMANISM
Being good without God and religion

HISTORICAL SETTING

In 1983, John Dunphy, a university graduate, entered a writing contest sponsored by *The Humanist* magazine. Dunphy, being one of 300 contestants, placed third. His article was titled, "A Religion for a New Age." Regarding the importance of teachers in the emergence of this new religion, namely humanism, he wrote: "I am convinced that the battle for mankind's future must be waged and won in the public school by *teachers who correctly perceive their role as the proselytizers of a new faith, a religion of humanity*."[1]

Historically speaking, the first decisive step in the realization of Dunphy's dream began in 1957. It was set in motion by *The Toronto Star*'s large headline on Saturday, October 5, of that year: "REDS LAUNCH 'MOON' TO CIRCLE WORLD." Russia had just launched Sputnik I—the world was awestruck!

This startling technological advance sent the West reeling. To many Americans, especially those involved in education, the ascent

---

1   John Dunphy, "A Religion for a New Age," *The Humanist* 43 (Jan/Feb 1983): 26. Author's italics.

of Sputnik had come "to symbolize a turning point;"[2] this incredible Russian achievement indicated the failure of the American science curriculum to keep pace with the changing times.

Hermann Muller (1890–1967), Professor of Biology at Indiana University and the recipient of the 1946 Nobel Prize in Medicine, wrote in 1959 that he was delighted to see that the Russian Sputnik program had awakened "the realization we must put new life into our science teaching."[3] Furthermore, he stated that the mandatory inclusion of evolutionary instruction should be foremost, especially in the science textbooks.

Two programs—the Biological Science Curriculum Study (BSCS) and Man: A Course of Study (MACOS)—were set up at the cost of $11.8 million. The science program was chaired by H. Bentley Glass (1906–2005), a biology professor at Johns Hopkins University, while the elementary social studies was led by Jerome Bruner (b. 1915), a Harvard psychologist. The teaching of evolutionism was to be a cornerstone doctrine within both of these courses.

It is highly significant that two university professors were appointed to chair these programs. Since the teaching of evolutionism on the university level had played an integral role for almost half a century, it only seemed logical that university professors would provide leadership in developing new curricula for secondary and elementary schools.

In the early 1960s, the secondary schools of Ontario followed their American counterparts by introducing evolutionism in both science and history textbooks.[4] Thus, from the early 60s until the present, the teaching of evolutionism has become

---

2 Peter Dow, *Schoolhouse Politics: Lessons from the Sputnik Era* (Cambridge: Harvard University Press, 1991), 30.

3 Hermann Muller, "One Hundred Years Without Darwinism Are Enough," *The Humanist* 19 (July 1959): 143.

4 For a detailed account of the growth of evolutionary content in history textbooks, see the author's doctoral thesis, "The Question of Human Origins: The Changing Context of Approved Ancient History Textbooks in Ontario 1846–1992" (Ed.D., diss., University of Toronto, 1992).

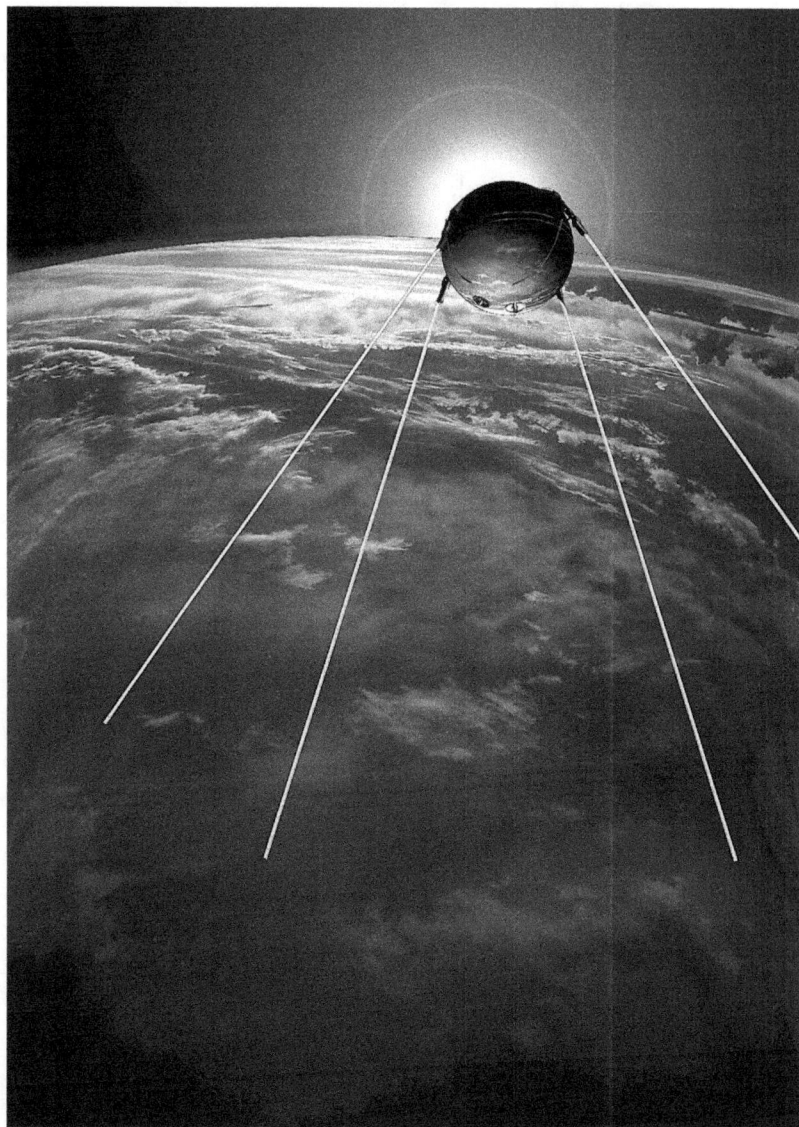

Sputnik I was launched by the Russians on October 4, 1957. It sent shockwaves throughout the West. This is an artist's impression of Sputnik I in orbit. (Image: Gregory R. Todd)

foundational for all secondary school curricula in both the United States and Canada.

In Ontario, the case of *Canadian Civil Liberties Association v. Minister of Education* (1990) concerning the teaching of the Bible during class time was heard, and the court ruled in favour of the plaintiff. Consequently, a new policy concerning religious training within Ontario schools was implemented; it was termed, "Education about Religion in the Public Elementary and Secondary Schools." Three germane stipulations were:

1. The school may sponsor the *study* of religion, but may not sponsor the *practice* of religion.
2. The school's approach is one of *instruction*, not one of *indoctrination*.
3. The school should strive for student *awareness* of all religions, but should not press for student *acceptance* of any one religion.[5]

The humanists, having successfully witnessed the removal of Christian influence from public education, had one more hurdle to leap over—the legitimization and acceptance of homosexuality/lesbianism as a normal lifestyle.[6]

The greatest impetus in achieving their goal occurred on July 19, 2005, when the Canadian government enacted Bill C-38 which officially legalized same-sex marriages. Six years later, the Toronto District School Board (TDSB)—the largest in Ontario—introduced, "Challenging Homophobia and Heterosexism: A K-12 Curriculum Resource Guide." Appendix B, a memorandum to all principals, states: "It is important to note that no student can be

---

5 Ontario Ministry of Education, "Part A: Introduction—History of Religious Education in Ontario Schools" in *Education About Religion in Ontario Public Elementary Schools* (1994)" (see http://www.edu.gov.on.ca/eng/document/curricul/religion/religioe.html#PartA; accessed May 2, 2014). Italics were in the original.

6 *Humanist Manifesto 2000: A Call for New Planetary Humanism*, drafted by Paul Kurtz (Amherst: Prometheus, 2000), 44–45.

exempted from Human Rights Education."[7] Any parental objection to the teaching of homosexuality/lesbianism on religious grounds would be denied. In other words, human rights education would always trump religious rights and freedoms.

There is absolutely no doubt that humanism has total control of the North American public education system from the primary grades to the Ph.D. level. But one should not forget that universities, totally committed humanistic institutions, are graduating our teachers, doctors, nurses, lawyers, judges and, most of all, our politicians—all of whom have been educated to assume "the role as the proselytizers of a new faith, a religion of humanity."[8]

THE FATHER OF SECULAR HUMANISM

Before the "New Atheists" went mainstream, it's arguable that [Paul] Kurtz did more to spread Humanism and skepticism than anyone else in modern history. If you read books written by Christian apologists prior to the year 2000, their enemy-in-chief wasn't Sam Harris or Richard Dawkins or Christopher Hitchens. It was Paul Kurtz.[9]

This tribute, given a day after his death, highlighted the impact that Paul Kurtz (1925–2012), the father of secular humanism, had during his lifetime. He was born into a Jewish family in Newark, New Jersey. Throughout his illustrious career, he authored 50 books and some 800 articles, which have been translated into 60 languages. Just prior to his eighteenth birthday in 1943,

---

7   Toronto District School Board, "Challenging Homophobia and Heterosexism: A K-12 Curriculum Guide" (2011), 212; http://gsanetwork.ca/sites/default/files/resources/ Challenging_Homophobia_and_Heterosexism:_A_K-12_Curriculum_Resource_Guide/ Challenging%20Homophobia%20and%20Heterosexism-A%20Resource%20Guide_0. pdf; accessed May 2, 2014.

8   Dunphy, "A Religion for a New Age": 26.

9   Hemant Mehta, "Paul Kurtz has died," *Friendly Atheist* (October 21, 2012); http:// www.patheos.com/blogs/friendlyatheist/2012/10/21/paul-kurtz-has-died/; accessed May 2, 2014.

he enlisted in the American army and was sent to Europe to fight against Nazi Germany.

His unit participated in the liberation of France, Belgium and Holland. In Germany, young Kurtz witnessed firsthand the atrocities in the Nazi concentration camps at Dachau and Buchenwald. "It was an experience that would be seared in his memory for the rest of his life."[10]

After the war, he resumed his university studies. In 1952, he was granted his doctorate in philosophy from Columbia University. After having taught philosophy at three universities, he accepted a position in 1965 at the State University of New York in Buffalo. For the next twenty-six years, he would present his humanistic philosophy to his students.

Two years after moving to Buffalo, this flag-bearer for humanism became editor of *The Humanist* magazine. During his ten-year tenure as editor, he was involved in two important ventures. First, he established Prometheus Publishing Company in 1969. From its inception, his mission as the chief editor was "to cultivate reason, science, humanistic values, and free inquiry in all areas of human interest."[11] Four decades later, his company had published 3,000 volumes from an atheistic persuasion.[12]

Second, he co-authored with Edwin Wilson the *Humanist Manifesto II* in 1973. This document, translated into seventy languages, was to become the most widely read publication of Prometheus Books. Living in the last quarter of the twentieth century, both Drs. Kurtz and Wilson were confident that the *Humanist Manifesto II* would provide a viable and much-needed

---

10 Jill Maxick, "Paul Kurtz, Publisher, Public Intellectual, and 'Father of Secular Humanism,' Dies at 86," Prometheus Books (October 20, 2012); http://www.prometheus-books.com/public/PKAnnouncement.html; accessed May 2, 2014.

11 "Prometheus Books: One-Third of a Century Young and Still Going Strong! An open letter from Paul Kurtz, Publisher and Founder"; http://www.independentpublisher.com/newsdetail.php?page=665; accessed May 2, 2014.

12 Paul Kurtz, *Multi-Secularism: A New Agenda* (New Brunswick: Transaction Publishers, 2010), 247.

Paul Kurtz (1925–2012) is considered the father and flag-bearer of secular humanism. He drafted the *Humanist Manifesto II* and established the Prometheus Publishing Company in 1969, which has, to date, published over 3,000 volumes.

religious alternative "that could serve present-day needs and guide humankind toward the future."[13]

The topic of religion came under discussion. The framers of the *Manifesto* acknowledged that "religion may inspire dedication to the highest ethical ideals."[14] True to humanist conviction, they clearly stated: "As non-theists, we begin with humans not God, nature not deity."[15]

Wanting to disassociate himself from any perceived negativity related to atheism, Dr. Kurtz began to promote secular humanism; it was to be viewed as being neither anti-religious nor religious.[16] Secular humanism was rather a methodology, supported by science and reason, that can evaluate "all truth claims, whether arising in popular belief, scientific theories or in moral, political, or religious claims."[17]

To strengthen his new resolve, Paul Kurtz wrote *Living without Religion: Eupraxsophy* in 1989. By combining three Greek words: *eu* (good), *praxis* (action) and *sophia* (wisdom), he coined a word meaning "good practical wisdom." Eupraxsophy—a convenient neologism—was to become the ethical and moral foundation for secular humanism. Historian Bill Cook, himself a humanist, has correctly stated:

> Kurtz has gone to great lengths to demonstrate the humanist ethics are independent of theistic ones. One can be awed by the beauty of the universe, love life to distraction, find fulfillment in other people, and live openly and

---

13 Paul Kurtz, ed., *Humanist Manifestos I and II* (Buffalo: Prometheus, 1973), 13.

14 Kurtz, ed., *Humanist Manifestos I and II*, 15.

15 Kurtz, ed., *Humanist Manifestos I and II*, 15.

16 For an opposing view, see the article by Edwin H. Wilson, a fellow friend and humanist, "The Origins of Modern Humanism," *The Humanist* 5 (January/February 1991): 9–11, 28. He clearly states that secular humanism is religious.

17 R. Joseph Hoffman, "The Secular Core of Humanism by Paul Kurtz," *The New Oxonian* (2011); http://rjosephhoffmann.wordpress.com/2011/03/29/the-secular-core-of-humanism-by-paul-kurtz; accessed May 2, 2014.

actively without being religious, and it was the intention of eupraxsophy.[18]

Certainly by 2011, Kurtz's definition of secular humanism, as being non-religious and moral without theistic overtones, had been adopted by a growing proportion of society, particularly in academia. But this humanist visionary was still faced with a very pressing challenge. The ever-vocal and aggressive "new atheists," such as Richard Dawkins (b. 1941) and Christopher Hitchens (1949–2011) were greatly tarnishing Kurtz's positive, respectful and dignified image of secular humanism within the eyes of the general public.

To counteract what he considered the acerbic attitude of his fellow atheists, the father of secular humanism penned *Neo-Humanism Statement of Secular Principles and Values* (2011). "Neo-Humanism" (another newly coined term) was designed to be highly inclusive in order to unite people worldwide to solve problems nationally and globally. Professor Kurtz was firmly convinced that this "softer and more gentle" approach would have greater appeal to the 16% (some 50 million Americans) who are not in some way connected to a church, temple or mosque.[19]

David Noebel, the founder of Summit Ministries, was one individual who was totally opposed to Kurtz's claims concerning secular humanism. In his book, *Clergy in the Classroom: The Religion of Secular Humanism*, he demonstrated from a historical perspective that the true nature of humanism and its more recent counterpart—secular humanism—was religious to the core.[20]

---

18 Bill Cooke, *A Wealth of Insights: Humanist Thought Since the Enlightenment* (Amherst: Prometheus, 2011), 198.

19 Paul Kurtz, *Neo-Humanist Statement of Secular Principles and Values* (Amherst: Prometheus, 2011), 52.

20 David Noebel, et al., *Clergy in the Classroom: The Religion of Secular Humanism*, rev. 2nd ed. (Manitou Springs: Summit Press, 2001). See also Judge W. Brevard Hand, *American Education on Trial: Is Secular Humanism a Religion?* (Cumberland: Center for Judicial Studies, 1987). During the trial, Judge Hand heard testimony from secular humanists, including Paul Kurtz, but he was not convinced that secular humanism was not religious.

Regardless of Paul Kurtz's literary subterfuge, humanism, by any name, has had a long religious tradition.

PAUL KURTZ'S VIEWS ON IMMORTALITY

"There is no credible evidence that life survives the death of the body,"[21] was stated by Paul Kurtz in the *Humanist Manifesto II*, written in 1973. This dedicated secular humanist maintained that, as a result of the evolutionary process, he "was composed of recycled stardust to which [he] would eventually return."[22] Death—the cessation of all human consciousness—is the final destination for everyone; consequently, immortality, premised upon a fictitious hope, is utterly absurd.

Samuel Magombo, a secular humanist from Malawi, Africa, contended that, upon becoming an atheist, he had had no difficulty in dispensing with the existence of God or the notion that the universe, and indeed life itself, had any meaning. But "of all the renunciations along the path towards atheism, giving up immortality hurt the most."[23]

Both Kurtz and Magombo agreed everyone's main preoccupation should be directed not on the life to come but on the here and now. Those who do not focus on the present *"lack the audacity to create their own world of hopes."*[24] Such a statement could not be said of Dr. Kurtz. After his death on October 22, 2012, lengthy memorials and tributes were written indicative of his highly productive and influential life.

To some, his two *Manifestos*, one in 1973 and the other in 2000, highlighted his brilliance and creativity. These documents clearly

---

21 Kurtz, ed., *Humanist Manifestos I and II*, 17.

22 Kurtz, *Multi-Secularism*, 43.

23 Samuel Magombo, "Is There Life After Death? The Humanist Response," Association for Secular Humanism in Malawi (August 31, 2010); http://secularhumanismmalawi.wordpress.com/2010/08/31/is-there-life-after-death-the-humanist-response/; no longer online May 2, 2014.

24 Paul Kurtz, "The Eupraxsophy of Hope," Council for Secular Humanism (December 7, 2012); http://www.secularhumanism.org/index.php?section=library&page=-kurtz_30_2; accessed June 2, 2014. Italics in the original.

articulated his humanistic sentiments and became the guideposts for the secular humanist movement. For others, their accolades centred on his establishment of the Centers for Inquiry as his greatest legacy. Through his indefatigable efforts, these centres could be found, not only in North America, but in Europe, Africa, India and also China. In Canada alone, there are ten branches. Their mandate is to provide both literary and human resources in the promotion of the ideals of secular humanism.

Unfortunately, there is a definite downside in having one's lasting legacy based upon people's remembrance or through one's positive contributions to society. By nature, everyone possesses human frailties. Kurtz was no exception. With the organizations that he personally founded, he wanted to have total control. A day after his death, *The Washington Post* featured an article written by Herb Silverman, the Distinguished Professor of Mathematics at the College of Charleston and a dynamic defender of humanism. He wrote a glowing tribute to Paul Kurtz, but he did make this candid and forthright observation:

> In my mind, Paul's greatest weakness was his less than enthusiastic willingness to play well with others. When I helped found the Secular Coalition for America in 2002, Kurtz wanted no part in it. He tended to view with suspicion organizations that *he did not lead or create*.[25]

At the end of the twentieth century, humanism has pervaded every avenue of life in the Western world. But it also has established the ideal religious climate to be supplanted by a close first-cousin—transhumanism.

---

25 Herb Silverman, "Remembering Paul Kurtz," *Washington Post* (October 23, 2012); http://www.faithstreet.com/onfaith/2012/10/23/remembering-paul-kurtz/10634; accessed May 2, 2014. Author's italics.

```
├────────┼────────┼────────■■■■■■■■■├
  1700     1800     1900     2000
```

05

TRANSHUMANISM
Becoming God

JULIAN HUXLEY'S DREAM

Julian Huxley (1887–1975), the grandson of Thomas Huxley, first coined the term transhumanism in 1957. In his book, *New Bottles for New Wine*, Dr. Huxley titled the introductory chapter, "Transhumanism." In the second-last paragraph, he outlined its potential by stating:

> The human species can, if it wishes, transcend itself—not just sporadically, an individual here in one way, an individual there in another way, but in its entirety, as humanity. We need a name for this new belief. Perhaps *transhumanism* will serve: man remaining man, but transcending himself, by realizing new possibilities of and for his human nature.[1]

---

1   Julian Huxley, *New Bottles for New Wine* (London: Chatto & Windus, 1959, 1957), 17. Italics in the original.

Sir Julian Huxley, a religious humanist, as witnessed in his book *Religion without Revelation*, confidently predicted that humanism would indeed become the prevailing worldview in the West.[2] In 1973, he was one of the signatories of *Humanist Manifesto II*. The declaration's oft-quoted statement, "No deity will save us; we must save ourselves,"[3] resonated strongly with this British visionary.

MOVING BEYOND SECULAR HUMANISM

In his *Humanist Manifesto 2000: A Call for a New Planetary Humanism*, Paul Kurtz articulated the purpose of the document in his concluding chapter:

> We alone are responsible for our own destiny, and the best we can do is to muster our intelligence, courage, and compassion to realize our highest aspirations. We believe that a good life is possible for each and every person of the planetary society of the future. Life can be meaningful for those willing to assume responsibility and undertake the cooperative efforts necessary to fulfill its promise. *We can and ought to create a new world of tomorrow.*[4]

Philosopher Max More (b. 1964), author of "Transhumanism: Towards a Futurist Philosophy," acknowledged that secular humanism had laid the historical foundation for transhumanism. But, in the first philosophical article concerning transhumanism, Dr. More stated that "Humanism, while a major step in the right direction, contained too many outdated values and ideas."[5] Specifically, his opposition to secular humanism was two-fold.

---

2 Julian Huxley, *Religion without Revelation*, rev. ed. (first published: 1927; New York: Harper & Brothers, 1957).

3 Paul Kurtz, ed., *Humanist Manifestos I and II* (Buffalo: Prometheus, 1973), 16.

4 *Humanist Manifesto 2000: A Call for New Planetary Humanism*, drafted by Paul Kurtz (Amherst: Prometheus, 2000), 63. Italics not in original.

5 Max More, "Transhumanism: Towards a Futurist Philosophy" (1990, 1996); http://www.maxmore.com/transhum.htm; this link no longer works, May 2, 2014.

First, he could see no value in expending time or resources on global or planetary humanism in which efforts are made "to rely exclusively on educational and cultural refinements to improve human nature."[6] Second, and more in tune with the transhumanist agenda, he had absolutely no sympathy for secular humanism's aversion to changing *Homo sapiens* into post-human beings. His transhumanist motto was:

> No more gods, no more faith, no more timid holding back. Let us blast out of our old forms, our ignorance, our weakness and our mortality. The future belongs to posthumanity.[7]

FM–2030

Noted transhumanist William Sims Bainbridge (b. 1940) paid tribute to Fereidoun M. Esfandiary (1930–2000) who, as a pioneer futurist in the 1970s, "had been propagandizing for technological transcendence."[8] Esfandiary envisioned that transhumanisn, also known as humanity plus ($h+$), could provide human enhancements that had, in the past, been relegated to science fiction. It would not only dominate every dimension of a person's life, but, for the first time in human history, the elimination of diseases, aging, and eventually even death, was on the horizon. An individual re-engineered through the process of transhumanism would have the capability of becoming a post-human or a cyborg (cybernetic organism).

Son of an Iranian diplomat, young Esfandiary, fluent in Arabic, French, Hebrew and English, lived in seventeen countries during the first eleven years of his life. "He said the experience influenced

---

6 Max More, "The Philosophy of Transhumanism," in *The Transhumanist Reader: Classical and Contemporary Essays on Science, Technology and Philosophy of the Human Future,* eds. Max More and Natasha Vita-More (Chichester: Wiley-Blackwell, 2013), 4.

7 Max More, "On Becoming Posthuman" (1994); http://eserver.org/courses/spring98/76101R/readings/becoming.html; accessed May 2, 2014.

8 William Sims Bainbridge, *Across the Secular Abyss: From Faith to Wisdom* (Lanham: Lexington, 2007), 223.

him to think of himself as a global citizen."[9] He emigrated to the United States to attend the University of California at Berkeley from which he graduated in 1952.

During 1959 to 1966, Esfandiary wrote three novels which were translated into twelve languages. His fictional writings featured the desperate need to eliminate worldwide political, national and racial barriers. But what was the human solution to end the heart-wrenching conditions of poverty, suffering and the devastation caused by wars? For the middle-aged Esfandiary, transhumanism offered the only viable option.

In 1989, this renowned visionary wrote, *Are You a Transhuman?* Its goal was to demonstrate that "a transhuman was a 'transitional human,' whose use of technology, way of living, and values" provided the means to become posthuman.[10] The material for the book was based upon his seminar notes gathered from 1969 to 1991 in a course he taught at the University of California Extension School, Los Angeles, titled: "Major Transformations: The Next Twenty Years."

The book was composed of twenty-five self-evaluation tests, such as: How future oriented are you? What is your level of humanity? How immortality oriented are you? His final test was: How transhuman are you?[11] These self-tests were designed to increase a person's awareness of transhumanism and the prospect of it becoming the next stage in human development.

A year before the book was published, F.M. Esfandiary legally changed his name to FM-2030—meaning Future Man of 2030. During a promotional tour for his book, FM-2030 was asked on *Larry King Live* why he had adopted this new name. He replied:

---

9   Douglas Martin, "Futurist Known as FM-2030 Is Dead at 69," *The New York Times* (July 11, 2000); http://www.nytimes.com/2000/07/11/us/futurist-known-as-fm-2030-is-dead-at-69.html; accessed May 2, 2014.

10   More and Vita-More, eds., *The Transhumanist Reader*, 11.

11   FM-2030, *Are You a Transhuman? Monitoring and Stimulating Your Personal Rate of Growth in a Rapidly Changing World* (New York: Warner Books, 1989).

FM-2030 (1930–2000) being interviewed on *Larry King Live* in 1989 while on a promotional tour of his book, *Are You a Transhuman?*

I am a person not involved in the past; I see myself as someone who lives in the future. I wanted a name that evokes the future. It is a name that evokes my dreams, hopes and visions. 2030 was a unique name. Forty years from now, one can expect life extension, space colonization, solar satellites, the ability to change the seasons and to have sunlight any time or anywhere. All these things will have been crystallized by then.[12]

FM-2030's book contained some remarkable predictions which, one must remember, were made in 1989. In his second

12 "Larry King Interviews Futurist FM-2030" (1989); http://www.youtube.com/watch?v=XkMVzEft7Og; accessed May 2, 2014.

self-test, he foresaw, "telemedicine...telenetwork, telebanking, teleshopping, telecommuting, teleconferencing."[13] More than two decades later, all of these have become commonplace.

His dream of being more advanced, more evolved by the year 2030, came crashing down when FM-2030 died of pancreatic cancer on July 11, 2000. His body was cryopreserved and placed in the Alcor Life Extension Foundation in Scottsdale, Arizona.

WATSON WINS JEOPARDY!

"Computer Wins on 'Jeopardy!': Trivial, It's Not," read the headline on February 16, 2011.[14] The victory of "Watson," named after IBM's first president, has given further credence to the predictions made by FM-2030 in the 1990s. This supercomputer had defeated two highly talented opponents, Ken Jennings (b. 1974) and Brad Rutter (b. 1978). Jennings had been victorious in 74 consecutive *Jeopardy!* games.

Since Deep Blue defeated chess grandmaster, Gary Kasparov (b. 1963) in 1997, IBM's executives had been looking for another challenge. In 2004, they chose the popular game show *Jeopardy!*, hosted by Alex Trebek (b. 1940).

In 2007, David Ferrucci (b. 1962), who had graduated with his doctorate in computer science from the Rensselaer Polytechnic Institute and directed the Semantic Analysis and Integration Department at IBM since 1995, accepted the position as principal program director for the project. Throughout the four-year research period, he was assisted by twenty to twenty-five people who had expertise in a variety of disciplines.

Both IBM and *Jeopardy!* producers believed that Watson should not be connected to the Internet as it definitely would have provided an unfair advantage over the two contestants. Instead, its 200 million pages of information were stored in eight data panels,

---

13 FM-2030, *Are You a Transhuman?*

14 John Markoff, "Computer Wins on 'Jeopardy!': Trivial, It's Not," *The New York Times* February 16, 2011); http://www.nytimes.com/2011/02/17/science/17jeopardy-watson. html?pagewanted=all&_r=1&; accessed May 2, 2014.

each the size of a refrigerator. Not only could Watson retrieve data instantaneously, but it was not plagued with the problem of forgetting material.

Interviewed some time after the victory, Dr. Ferrucci was asked what he found to be the most challenging aspect of the *Jeopardy!* project.[15] His response was that programming Watson proved to be the most difficult, given that it needed to understand natural language with all its nuances and complexities.

Asked what benefits this four-year project could offer to the general public, Ferrucci suggested that one possible area would be in the field of medicine. He envisioned either a nurse or a physician could ask Watson for a specific diagnosis. Since medical literature is expanding at an ever-increasing rate, the IBM computer has the capability, with blazing speed, to search through the most current literature and report back to the health practitioner with a variety of optional treatments.

Two years after the *Jeopardy!* challenge, "Watson has become 240% faster and 75% smaller. Watson can now run on a single server, which is the size of four stacked pizza boxes, onsite or through the cloud."[16] Is it any wonder that Larry Norton (b. 1947), a renowned oncologist at the Memorial Sloan-Kettering Cancer Center, has praised the capabilities of Watson as becoming an indispensable partner for all medical personnel. Since medical information concerning cancer treatment and genetic research is doubling every five years, he noted that Watson was "more than a machine. Computer science is going to evolve rapidly and medicine will evolve with it."[17]

But other areas, such as financial institutions and government, are also benefiting from the astounding advances in computer

---

15 David Ferrucci interviewed by Nikola Danaylov on *Singularity 1 on 1*; "Pursue the Big Challenges"; http://www.singularityweblog.com/david-ferrucci-on-singularity-1-on-1-pursue-the-big-challenges/; accessed May 2, 2014.

16 Martin Kohn, "Beyond 'Jeopardy!': What's Watson Up To Now?," *Huffington Post* (June 27, 2013); http://www.huffingtonpost.com/dr-matin-kohn/ibm-beyond-jeopardy-whats-ibm_b_3466032.html; accessed May 2, 2014.

17 Kohn, "Beyond 'Jeopardy!'"

technology. From its inception during World War II, when the codebreakers in Blechley Park invented the forerunner of modern computers to decipher Nazi messages,[18] the computer now dominates every aspect of life. "For example, John Donoghue's research team at Brown University has developed a technology that enables quadriplegics to read e-mails, control a television, turn a light on and off and play video games using their minds."[19]

Paul Kurtz' vision that secular humanism would resolve problems, nationally and globally, for all intents and purposes perished with him at his death in 2012. Transhumanist and author Simon Young (b. 1964) has articulated a different vision. "As [secular] humanism freed us from the chains of superstition, let transhumanism free us from our biological chains."[20] Such freedom, as understood by Young, can only occur when humanity takes the reins of evolutionary development under its own control.

MOVING BEYOND DARWINISM

In his "Apologia for Transhumanist Religion," Gregory Jordan defined transhumanism as a comprehensive worldview which sought to explain "the origin and destiny of the universe, and the inner, subjective life of human beings."[21] In other words, this religious perspective, as is true of all religions, provided answers to the three eternal questions of life: Where did we come from? Why are we here? Where are we going?[22]

18 See B. Jack Copeland, ed., *Colossus: The Secrets of Bletchley Park's Codebreaking Computers* (Oxford: Oxford University Press, 2006).

19 Robert M. Geraci, "Cyborgs, Robots and Eternal Avatars: Transhumanist Salvation at the Interface of Brains and Machines" in *The Routledge Companion to Religion and Science*, ed. James W. Haag, Gregory R. Peterson and Michael L. Spezio (London: Routledge, 2012), 582.

20 Simon Young, *Designer Evolution: A Transhumanist Manifesto* (Amherst: Prometheus, 2005), 32.

21 Gregory Jordan, "Apologia for Transhumanist Religion," *Journal of Evolution and Technology*, 15 (1) (February 2006): 60.

22 See the author's *Eternity Before Their Eyes, Worldviews Examined: The Apostle Paul in Athens and Modern University Students* (London: D & I Herbert, 2007). 1,200 students were interviewed off campus at the University of Western Ontario for their opinions concerning these three questions.

Concerning the first question, transhumanists concur that the universe and life itself came into existence by natural forces. A Creator of any description does not exist. Thus, all life has developed through eons of time by an evolutionary process. By means of superior intelligence, humans—a highly developed animal—have become the apex of evolutionary development. To survive as a species, they had "to reshape the natural, social and political environments in which they live, while also transforming themselves within those environments."[23]

Noting that humanity has moved beyond biological evolutionism, some sociologists have termed the next stage as cultural evolutionism. Francis Fukuyama, an American political scientist and author of *Our Posthuman Future: Consequences of the Biotechnology Revolution* (2002), called transhumanism "the 'Most Dangerous Idea in the World'."[24] Dr. Fukuyama greatly feared that technology in the hands of transhumanists would alter the natural course of cultural evolutionism. He felt that as technology advanced, it should be regulated in order to protect the rights and dignity of all humanity.

On the other hand, Leon Klass, trained as a physician and biochemist, and chairman of the President's Council on Bioethics from 2001 to 2005, found transhumanism to be utterly repugnant. "A quest for immortality or greatly extended life spans necessarily imperils the mortality and finitude from which meaning and virtue are derived."[25]

In spite of humanity's achievements, transhumanists have been very critical of the physical limitations placed upon them by evolutionism. Allan Buchanan has clearly expressed his utter contempt for the process of human evolutionism:

---

23 Brent Waters, *This Mortal Flesh: Incarnation and Bioethics* (Grand Rapids: Brazos, 2009), 24.

24 Kyle Munkittrick, "The Most Dangerous Idea in the World," *Discover* magazine blog (September 15, 2010); http://blogs.discovermagazine.com/sciencenotfiction/2010/09/15/the-most-dangerous-idea-in-the-world/; accessed May 14, 2014.

25 Waters, *This Mortal Flesh*, 101.

The human organism is not a finely balanced whole because evolution did not create harmonious, "complete"
organisms; instead it produced tentative, changing,
perishing, cobbled-together *ad hoc* solutions to transient
design problems, with blithe disregard for human
well-being. Nature was not wise (or unwise) and *evolution
is not like a Master Engineer*; it is more like a morally
insensitive, blind, tightly shackled tinkerer.[26]

Loathing of the human body leads directly into the second
question of this secular worldview: Why are we here? Dr. Jordan's
response was: "Transhumanism is characterized by belief in the
'possibility and desirability' of developing advanced technologies
to 'improve the human condition.'"[27] Having a deep-seated faith
in human capabilities, these futurists envision that individuals
will be able to orchestrate the changes that are necessary to build
a better life.

Transhumanists, as do humanists, have long contended that
people have a solely materialistic existence. Thus, no one possesses
a spirit. Although not a transhumanist, Francis Crick (1916–2004),
co-discoverer of the structure of the DNA molecule in 1953, believed the spirit was "a group of neurons; that what people regarded as the human spirit was actually a component of the brain."[28]

In 2002, a report, *Converging Technologies for Improving Human
Performance*, was published by the National Science Foundation
in America. Its goal was to explore "the synergistic combination
of four major 'NBIC' (nano-bio-info-cogno) provinces of science
and technology, each of which is currently progressing at a rapid
rate."[29]

---

26 Allen E. Buchanan, *Beyond Humanity? The Ethics of Biomedical Enhancement* (Oxford: Oxford University Press, 2011), 2. Author's italics.

27 Jordan, "Apologia for Transhumanist Religion": 62. Italics not in the original.

28 Brian Alexander, *Rapture: How Biotech Became the New Religion* (New York: Basic Books, 2003), 13.

29 Mihail C. Roco and William Sims Bainbridge, eds., *Converging Technologies for Improving Human Performance: Nanotechnology, Biotechnology, Information Technology and*

There has always been the expectation that, in a very short time span, this tetradic convergence of nanotechnology, biotechnology, information technology and cognitive science could offer humanity a greater sense of autonomy in making life choices. In its wake, everyone would be expected to be healthier and to have happier and longer lives. This rationale has always been at the core of NBIC.[30]

Since the thirteen-year project of mapping of the human genome was completed in 2003, attention has now focused on the human mind—now considered the "last biological frontier." To understand how the mind functions, these scientific futurists have adopted a procedure called reverse-engineering. Their plan is to construct a brain which will emulate human intelligence and consciousness. Some of these visionaries see the day when "uploading"—sending information from the brain into "stronger and more flexible mechanical substrates"[31]—will not be considered outlandish but a commonplace exercise.

At the White House on April 2, 2013, President Barack Obama (b. 1961) made this extremely important announcement:

> The next great American project is what we are calling the BRAIN initiative. As humans, we can identify galaxies light years away; we can study particles smaller than atoms, but we still haven't unlocked the mystery of the three pounds of matter between our ears. Today scientists possess the capability to study individual neurons...a human brain contains almost 100 billion neurons, making trillions of connections.[32]

Cognitive Science (NSF/DOC-sponsored report, June 2002); http://www.wtec.org/ConvergingTechnologies/1/NBIC_report.pdf; accessed May 14, 2014.

30 Dónal P. O'Mathúna, Nanoethics: Big Ethical Issues with Small Technology (London: Continuum, 2009), 167.

31 Ben Goertzel and Stephan Vladimir Bugaj, The Path to Posthumanity: 21st Century Technology and Its Radical Implications for Mind, Society and Reality (Bethesda: Academica, 2006), 217.

32 "Obama unveils brain mapping investment program," NBC News (April 2, 2013); http://www.nbcnews.com/video/nbc-news/51403644#51403644; accessed May 14, 2014.

Before the leaders of the American scientific community, the president promised $100 million to begin the mapping of the human brain. The research, he suggested, will make medical advances to either uncover new ways to treat or, better still, cure such diseases as Alzheimer's, Parkinson's, epilepsy and post-traumatic stress disorder, which has debilitated numerous war veterans. This announcement was greatly applauded by many Americans suffering from these disorders.

Furthermore, with an air of patriotic confidence, the president said: "We have been a nation of dreamers and risk-takers; people who see what nobody else sees sooner than anybody else sees it. We do innovation better than anybody else—and that makes our economy stronger."[33] To illustrate this point, he made reference to the mapping of the human genome.

To accomplish this extraordinary feat, the American government spent $3.8 billion over a period of thirteen years. But, for every dollar spent, the president reported, $140 has been earned. Thus, to date, a $3.8 billion investment has returned $532 billion! It is expected that the BRAIN project will cost about the same and hopefully yield the same profit rates. Each year for the next ten years, $300 million is being allocated for the BRAIN initiative. But, economically, "there are hopes that it could create thousands of jobs in spin-off scientific and technological enterprises."[34]

Across the continent in California, the co-founders of Google, Larry Page (b. 1973) and Sergey Brin (b. 1973), have been interested in artificial intelligence (AI) for some time. In their quest to forge ahead in AI research, their company has made some amazing advancements in Deep Learning. "Deep Learning software attempts to mimic the activity in layers of neurons in the neocortex, the wrinkly 80% of the brain where thinking occurs."[35]

---

33 "Obama Unveils Brain Mapping Investment Program," *NBC News* (April 2, 2013).

34 Sarah Boseley, "Obama Unveils Brain Mapping Initiative and Calls for Further Research," *The Guardian* (April 2, 2013); http://www.guardian.co.uk/science/2013/apr/02/obama-brain-initiative-fight-disease; accessed May 14, 2014.

35 Robert D. Hof, "10 Breakthrough Technologies 2013: Deep Learning," *MIT Technology Review* (April 23, 2013); http://www.technologyreview.com/featuredstory/513696/deep-learning/; accesssed May 14, 2014.

The University of Toronto announced on March 12, 2013, that Google had not only hired Geoffrey Hinton (b. 1947), Professor of Computer Science, and two of his graduate students, Alex Krizhevsky and Ilya Sutskever, but also purchased their company, DNNresearch. As a world renowned researcher in Deep Learning, Dr. Hinton has been given, from his perspective, the ideal situation: "He gets to stay in Toronto, splitting his time between Google and his teaching duties at the University of Toronto, while Krizhevsky and Sutskever fly south to work at Google's Mountain View, California campus."[36]

At the moment, it would appear that the American government (with its sponsorship of therapeutic research) and private enterprise (working at developing artificial intelligence) are focused on two separate areas; but it will be only a matter of time before their efforts will coalesce. Once the human brain is mapped, the transhumanists' dream of transcending to posthumanity will be, for the first time, a distinct possibility.

Transhumanists have maintained that natural selection, the Darwinian vehicle for change, has operated by means of slow, random and non-directed processes over millions of years. Now, having reached the twenty-first century, they have set a new path for human transcendence: "natural selection to *deliberate selection*; Darwinian evolutionism to *enhancement evolutionism*."[37]

THE MEDIA AND TRANSHUMANISM

During the first week of 2014, the television audience of North America witnessed the premiere broadcast of *Intelligence* on CBS. The network stated: "As the first supercomputer with a beating heart, Gabriel Vaughn [the star of the show] is the most valuable piece of technology the country has ever created and is the U.S.'s

---

36 Robert McMillan, "Google Hires Brains That Helped Supercharge Machine Learning," *Wired* (March 13, 2013); http://www.wired.com/wiredenterprise/2013/03/google_hinton/; accessed May 14, 2014.

37 John Harris, *Enhancing Evolution: The Ethical Case for Making Better People* (Princton: Princton University Press, 2010), 4. Author's italics.

secret weapon."[38] The thirteen episodes ran from January 7 until March 13, 2014.

Equipped with a high-powered computer chip in his head, this high-tech intelligence operative has access to the global information grid, such as the Internet, WiFi, telephone and satellite data, in his battle against international terrorism. The American Secret Service, realizing that Vaughn had a penchant for being daring and somewhat erratic, assigned Riley Neal, a female agent, to protect him. The male-female dynamic with all its human facets was designed to captivate the emotions of the viewing audience.

The last episode, "Being Human," centred around Vaughn's recovery from bullet wounds. His mother, a combat nurse, provided the medical expertise to accomplish this feat. The finalé not only stressed the humanity of this "intelligence operative," but concluded by introducing a high-ranking American politician who was covertly assisting foreign terrorists. This theatrical hook was to leave viewers with an anticipated sequel in the fall, but on May 10, 2014, CBS cancelled *Intelligence* after only one season. The Internet Movie Database (IMDb) gave it a rating of 7.2/10 from 8,433 users.[39]

In the wake of *Intelligence*, a science fiction movie based upon the singularity theory of Ray Kurzweil, the world's leading transhumanist,[40] was released in theatres on April 14, 2014. *Transcendence* stars Johnny Depp as Dr. Will Caster, a renowned artificial intelligence (AI) researcher, who has created a sentient machine that possesses amazing intellectual capabilities. In order to elude anti-technology extremists and impending death, he successfully uploads his own consciousness into his newly developed creation.

Caster's transcendence poses a serious dilemma for his wife and a close friend, both of whom are AI researchers. "This scientist

---

38 Tim Goodman, "*Intelligence*: TV Review," *The Hollywood Reporter* (January 7, 2014); http://www.hollywoodreporter.com/review/tv-review-cbs-intelligence-668880; accessed May 14, 2014.

39 "*Intelligence* (2014)," IMDb; http://www.imdb.com/title/tt2693776/; accessed May 14, 2014.

40 See chapter 6.

Intelligence (CBS TV series): Gabriel Vaughn (played by Josh Holloway) is equipped with a high-powered computer chip in his head.

quickly becomes intertwined with the Internet, giving him access to every electronic system on Earth, and is soon developing stunning breakthroughs that promise to change the planet for the better. But Will has other goals as well, and his growing power makes him a threat to anyone in his way."[41]

To engage the global public in discussing and accepting the possibility of the emergence of a posthumanist world the media's role will undoubtedly be profound. With secularism's ever-growing popularity, the posthumanist promise of granting immortality will become even more appealing.

CRYONICS—IMMORTALITY PENDING
Death, having plagued humanity throughout history, is "the end result of degeneration and morbidity."[42] Bolstered by the breathtaking advances in modern technology, transhumanists have set

---

41 "*Transcendence*: A Review," *Common Sense Media* (April 18, 2014); https://www.commonsensemedia.org/movie-reviews/transcendence; accessed May 14, 2014.

42 Waters, *This Mortal Flesh*, 95.

their sights on the elimination of death. Not believing in God or any type of afterlife, transhumanists contend that, until now, death has sent everyone into oblivion. But the war continues to be waged against this foe. Victory can only be attained by pressing forward to becoming posthuman and then, and only then, will immortality be fully realized.

ROBERT ETTINGER

In the meantime, advocates of transhumanism are presently dying! What interim step can be taken to preserve their bodies until that "grand moment" of immortality is achieved? As far back as 1964, Robert C.W. Ettinger (1918–2011), a physics teacher at Wayne State University, recommended cryonics in his book, *The Prospect of Immortality*. On the first page, he outlined what he considered the only viable option:

> *The fact:* At very low temperatures, it is possible, *right now*, to preserve dead people with essentially no deterioration, indefinitely. (Details and references will be supplied.)
> *The assumption:* If civilization endures, medical science should *eventually* be able to repair almost any damage to the human body, including freezing damage and senile debility or other causes of death. (Definite reasons for such optimism will be given.)[43]

James Bedford (1893–1967), a retired University of California psychology professor, became the first person to be cryonically preserved (frozen) after dying of cancer in 1967. The Cryonics Society of California informed the press that "when a cure for cancer was found, Dr. Bedford's body would be thawed and an attempt made to revive him."[44] Unfortunately, since cryopreservative

---

43 Robert C.W. Ettinger, *The Prospect of Immortality* (New York: Doubleday & Company, 1964), 1.

44 David Boyd Haycock, *Mortal Coil: A Short History of Living Longer* (New Haven: Yale University Press, 2008), 199.

Robert C.W. Ettinger (1918–2011) is considered the father of cryonics. He established the Cryonics Institute in Clinton, Michigan, in 1976, where his body is presently cryopreserved.

techniques were not well developed at that time, the family's concern about the care of his body became so heightened that they frequently had it moved from one facility to another. Finally, in 1982, Bedford's body was sent to the Alcor Life Extension Foundation in Scottsdale, Arizona, where it has remained ever since.

"Robert Ettinger, the father of cryonics, is gone—for now,"[45] reported *The Telegraph* on July 23, 2011. He was ninety-two years old. Confident that cryonics was indeed the first step in gaining immortality, Ettinger had established the Cryonics Institute in Clinton, Michigan, in 1976. Some thirty-five years later, he has now become the 106th patient to be cryopreserved in his own institution.

ALCOR LIFE EXTENSION FOUNDATION

The Alcor Life Extension Foundation has always been on the cutting edge of developing and improving cryopreservation. Max More, a vocal advocate of transhumanism, became its CEO in 2011. In describing the cost of being cryopreserved, Dr. More mentioned that there were two important costs.

The first is an annual membership fee of $620 in order to maintain organizational functions of the company. But the main cost, as outlined by More, "is the actual cryopreservation fee itself which allows us to do the whole procedure and keep the body cryopreserved for decades. That currently is a minimum of $200,000 for a whole patient or $80,000 for a neural [head only] patient."[46] To assist in defraying the cost of what he calls "the life extension option," individuals can establish a life insurance policy and make Alcor Life Extension Foundation their beneficiary.

In defence of the 119 people who have been cryopreserved at Alcor,[47] Max More made this interesting comment:

---

45 Rob Furber, "Robert Ettinger, the Father of Cryonics, is Gone—For Now," *The Telegraph* (August 9, 2011); http://www.telegraph.co.uk/science/8691489/Robert-Ettinger-the-father-of-cryonics-is-gone-for-now.html; accessed May 14, 2014.

46 Max More interviewed by Nikola Danaylov on *Singularity 1 on 1*; "Max More Interview," (August 8, 2013); http://www.youtube.com/watch?v=JoxiX9mPB_s; accessed May 14, 2014.

47 "Max More Interview," (August 8, 2013).

We'll look back on this 50 to 100 years from now — we'll shake our heads and say, "What were people thinking? They took these people who were very nearly viable, just barely dysfunctional, and they put them in an oven or buried them under the ground, when there were people who could have put them into cryopreservation." I think we'll look at this just as we look today at slavery, beating women, and human sacrifice, and we'll say, "This was insane — a huge tragedy."[48]

As expected, there have been many who have been very critical of cryonics. Arthur Rowe, the past editor-in-chief of *Cryobiology* (1972 to 1994) and Professor of Forensic Medicine at New York Medical School, has been a vocal critic of cryonics. In a television documentary interview, the United States' foremost cryobiologist frankly stated that people have been duped into believing what is totally unreasonable—that they can be kept in a frozen state and then revived. How could anyone believe in such a fantasy? To Dr. Rowe, it is hardly scientific and "borders on science fiction."[49] But his most notable and sternest comment was that "believing cryonics could reanimate somebody who has been frozen is like believing you can turn hamburger back into a cow."[50]

The title of Stephen Cave's book, *Immortality: The Quest to Live Forever and How it Drives Civilization*, bears testimony to the innate desire of civilizations (and individuals) to avoid death. He has even less confidence in cryonics—"a wonderful demonstration of human ingenuity in weaving an immortality narrative from scraps of science, myth and speculation."[51] But despite its

---

48 Aschwin de Wolf, "Cryonics: Using Low Temperatures to Care for the Critically Ill," Institute for Evidence Based Cryonics (2011); http://www.evidencebasedcryonics. org/what-is-cryonics/; accessed May 14, 2014.

49 "Stranger Than Fiction," Alcor Foundation (Cryonics) Part A (2006); http://www. youtube.com/watch?v=FX28Cg-z9kw; accessed May 14, 2014.

50 "Notable Quotes," Alcor Life Extension Foundation (2013); http://www.alcor.org/ notablequotes.html; accessed May 14, 2014. The citation dates back to at least 1989.

51 Stephen Cave, *Immortality: The Quest to Live Forever and How It Drives Civilization* (New York: Crown, 2012), 125.

lack of plausibility, transhumanists are more than willing to be cryopreserved. In their minds, it provides them the possibility, even if it is remote, of being revived in the future. Burial in the ground or cremation are truly "dead ends."

Since only 300 people have been cryopreserved in the United States over the last fifty years, cryonics has definitely not captured the hearts and imaginations of the American people. Being shunned by the scientific community as fraudulent, has only heightened its poor reception. But the image of cryonics is about to change.

"Meet Byron's Bionic Man," was the headline story in my local newspaper.[52] The caption itself had a nuance of transhumanism. Hit by an impaired driver while riding his bicycle, Mitch Brogan lost the use of his legs and arms. With $150,000 from his insurance claim, he has now been equipped with a robotic exoskeleton that enables him to walk. This amazing device is operated by 29 computers.

Astounding stories like this and many others are routinely reported by the media. Transhumanism, piggybacking on these feats of technology, is becoming more widely known. Its advocates, such as Ray Kurzweil, Aubrey de Grey (b. 1963) and Kevin Warwick (b. 1954), are gaining worldwide attention and have been provided with a platform to convey their message that humanity has within its grasp the capability of achieving immortality—finally, they can become gods. Surely, these men should be heralded as the god-makers!

---

52 "Meet Byron's Bionic Man," *The London Free Press* (Monday, April 30, 2012), A1.

06

RAY KURZWEIL
Transcendent man

A RELIGIOUS MAN

> The universe will wake up; it will become intelligent and
> that will multiply our intelligence trillions upon trillions.
> ...it is called the Singularity. But regardless what you call
> it, it will be the universe waking up. *Does God exist? I
> would say, "Not yet."*[1]

T hese words were uttered by Ray Kurzweil in the final
scene of *Transcendent Man: The Life and Ideas of Ray
Kurzweil* (2009). The religious views of the sixty-one-
year-old Kurzweil, as portrayed in the documentary,
have changed little from the time he was a young man.

Kurzweil was born in Queens, New York City, in 1948. His
secular Jewish parents were highly talented; his father was a

---

1 *Transcendent Man: The Life and Ideas of Ray Kurzweil.* Directed by Barry Ptolemy
(DVD, Ptolemic, 86 min., 2009). Author's italics.

musician/conductor and his mother, a visual artist. Both escaped
from Austria to the United States in 1938, prior to the Nazi reign
of terror in Europe. They instilled in their son "a veneration for
human creativity and the power of ideas"[2] which formed the basis
of the family religion.

During an interview, Ray Kurzweil recalled an incident which
truly epitomized his family's humanistic worldview.[3] When he
was eight years old, his grandfather, for the first time since he had
left Europe in 1938, paid a return visit in 1956. At that time, his
grandfather had the opportunity of personally holding the Codex
Leicester, a collection of the original scientific writings by
Leonardo da Vinci (1452–1519).[4] For a moment, he was overcome
with reverential awe.

More than half a century later, this "religious experience" of
his grandfather handling the illustrious codex still profoundly
affected Kurzweil as it spoke directly to his view of life. He
commented: "This was not something handed down by God;
this was a document that had been created by a human, but that
was the ultimate transcendence. A human being creating ideas
that ultimately changed the world."[5]

As a young man, he and his parents attended a Universalist
Unitarian Church in New York. The liberal theological stance of
social justice and respect for human life was appealing to the
Kurzweil family. The concept of tolerance was also exemplified in
the investigations of the beliefs of all the major religions in the
world. For a six-month period, each religion was studied and rep-
resentatives of each faith were invited to present their particular
viewpoint and then dialogue with church members. The main

---

2   Ray Kurzweil, *The Singularity Is Near: When Humans Transcend Biology* (New York: Viking, 2005), 1.

3   Ray Kurzweil interviewed by Nikola Danaylov on *Singularity 1 on 1*; "Be Who You Would Like To Be," (October 2012); http://www.singularityweblog.com/ray-kurzweil-on-singularity-1-on-1/; accessed May 14, 2014.

4   In 1994, Bill Gates purchased the collection of largely scientific writings for $34 million.

5   Kurzweil interviewed Danaylov, "Be Who You Would Like To Be."

theme gleaned by the teenage Kurzweil was that there were many paths to spiritual truth.

Writing an article in 2007 on his company's blog, law professor Michael Cohen, a leader in business and health care law, mentioned that both Senator Barak Obama, then campaigning for the American presidency, and Ray Kurzweil, were keynote speakers at the fiftieth anniversary celebration of the United Church of Christ in Hartford, Connecticut. He noted that both these influential public figures spoke "about the contribution of their religious upbringing to their distinctive social visions."[6]

Kurzweil's speech began by reminiscing about his religious education in the Unitarian Church. It was in this church that he "developed a life-long desire to keep learning about truth, a thirst for knowledge, and a way of living informed by the Golden Rule."[7] After demonstrating one of his inventions (a camera-sized device that could be used by a blind person to read printed material), he concluded by drawing a connection between faith and technology. By embracing them both, individuals would be equipped with a deeper understanding and appreciation for the world in which they live.

Pertaining to the question, "Where did we come from?" Dr. Kurzweil wrote: "Let us praise evolution[ism]. It has created a plethora of designs of indescribable beauty, complexity and elegance, not to mention effectiveness."[8] The origin of this matchless, intricate universe was a total mystery to him, but he was absolutely certain that God was not its Craftsman.

Kurzweil recognizes that many religious traditions are, in reality, very similar: they describe God as being unlimited in power,

---

6   Michael Cohen, "Kurzweil Obama Double-Header Showcases Religious Pluralism," *CamLaw: Complementary and Alternative Medicine Law Blog*; http://www.camlawblog.com/articles/spirituality-in-healthcare/kurzweil-obama-doubleheader-showcases-religious-pluralism/; accessed May 14, 2014.

7   Steve Dahlberg, "National Religious Gathering Explores Faith, Science, Creativity and Society," *Applied Imagination Blog* (June 24, 2007); http://appliedimagination.blogspot.ca/2007_06_01_archive.html; accessed May 14, 2014.

8   Ray Kurzweil, *The Age of Spiritual Machines: When Computers Exceed Human Intelligence* (New York: Viking, 1999), 44.

creativity, intelligence, memory and love. But according to Kurzweil, all these attributes are located within the human neocortex. But, from his religious perspective, as humanity evolved, these divine qualities had been evolving within the human species itself. Thus, "evolution[ism] is a spiritual process; entities become more god-like, never reaching that ideal but moving in that direction exponentially. So, we are going to explode into these very qualities in which God is described."[9]

In his seminal work, *The Singularity Is Near*, this scientist turned historian divided the entirety of world history—both biological and technological—from the distant past to the endless future into six epochs. Evolutionism, an undirected and random process, was the underlying thematic continuum throughout these epochs.

Epoch 1 witnessed the origin of "information in its basic structures: patterns of matter and energy."[10] From these primary forces, the evolutionary system was set in motion. But, with the emergence of transhumanism in Epoch 5, NBIC (nano-bio-info-cogno) technologies will be so advanced that humanity will be able to move beyond the long-awaited Singularity into Epoch 6. Possessing a total transformation of body and mind, post-humans will have the capability to venture beyond the earth. Then, as prophesied by Kurzweil, the universe would finally be alive!

Understanding the necessity for people to worship, this visionary believed that a new religion must be created. The major religions of the world must be disbanded, as their principal reason for existence has been "to rationalize the tragedy of death as a good thing."[11] Such a rationale was applicable in the past, but post-humanism could offer something more appealing—immortality.

---

9 "Ray Kurzweil: Human Enhancement and Singularity"; *Religion & Ethics News-Weekly* (July 15, 2011); http://www.youtube.com/watch?v=6XY38r9x5k4&feature=related; accessed May 14, 2014. See also Kurzweil interviewed by James Bedsole, "Ray Kurzweil on How We Will Become God-like," *33rd Square* (January 2, 2014); http://www.33rdsquare.com/2014/01/ray-kurzweil-on-how-we-will-become-god.html; accessed May 14, 2014.

10 Kurzweil, *The Singularity Is Near*, 14–21.

11 Kurzweil, *The Singularity Is Near*, 374.

Kurzweil foresaw the need for only two religious principles: the respect for human consciousness and knowledge.

AN INVENTOR AND HUMANITARIAN

"Was that thing written by a computer?" This question was asked of Raymond Kurzweil by panelist and film star, Henry Morgan, on the television program, *I've Got a Secret*.[12] The seventeen-year-old had played a melody on the piano that his computer had composed. After viewing the computer that this teenager had built, Steve Allen (1921–2000), the host of the show, made this prediction: "Raymond, I am astounded that anyone could do anything of this sort. I predict a great future for you."[13]

From the age of five, the precocious Kurzweil wanted to be an inventor. It was three years later that he built a robotic puppet theatre. From a command station, he was able to control all its movements. His classmates were enthralled with his novel creation. But the pivotal moment for this aspiring inventor came at the age of twelve. His uncle, an engineer at Bell Labs, taught him the basics of computer science.

After graduating from secondary school, Kurzweil decided to study computer science at the Massachusetts Institute of Technology (MIT) in 1965. There were two main reasons that he was attracted to this prestigious university. First, he would have the opportunity to study under Dr. Marvin Minsky (b. 1927) who had established the newly formed computer science program at MIT. Second, he was informed that, even as a student, he would be able to use the university's computer. An IBM 7094, costing $11 million (in today's dollars), it took up a good portion of a building and was used by students and professors alike. "Today, the computer in your cell phone is a million times smaller, a million times less expensive, and a thousand times more powerful."[14]

---

12 "Ray Kurzweil on *I've Got a Secret*" (1965); http://www.youtube.com/watch?v=X4Neivqp2K4; accessed May 14, 2014.

13 *Transcendent Man* (2009).

14 Ray Kurzweil and Terry Grossman, *Transcend: Nine Steps to Living Well Forever* (New York: Rodale, 2009), xiii.

In 1970, Kurzweil graduated with a B.Sc. degree in computer science. Four years later, he established his first major business, Kurzweil Computer Products Inc. His company developed a computer program that used the well-established Optical Character Recognition (OCR) that was able to convert any style of font into a readable format; hence, it was termed an Omni-Font OCR. The obvious question was: Where could such an invention be used?

Sitting beside a blind person on a flight, Kurzweil learned from him that a major handicap in his life was "his inability to read ordinary printed material."[15] Kurzweil's inventive mind envisaged how his Omni-Font OCR could provide a viable solution to this blind man's handicap. So, with the assistance of his colleagues, he developed two other new technologies—"the first CCD flat-bed scanner [and] the first full text-to-speech synthesizer."[16] With these three combined technologies, the first print-to-speech reading machine for the blind was created.

On January 13, 1976, Ray Kurzweil and leaders of the National Federation of the Blind held a press conference and introduced the Kurzweil Reading Machine to the public. "All the evening network news programs carried the story and Walter Cronkite (1916–2009) used the machine to read aloud his signature sign-off. 'And that's the way it was, January 3, 1976.'"[17]

Shortly after this nationwide announcement, Kurzweil was invited to appear on the *Today Show* to demonstrate his reading machine. Stevie Wonder (b. 1950), a blind singer-songwriter and record producer, happened to hear the show and bought the company's first manufactured unit.

An immediate friendship between the inventor and the musical superstar was established. In 1982, during a recording session in Los Angles, Stevie Wonder mentioned to Kurzweil that the acoustic musical instruments, such as the piano and guitar,

---

15 Kurzweil, *The Age of Spiritual Machines*, 174.

16 Kurzweil Technologies website, "A Brief Career Summary of Ray Kurzweil," (2014); http://www.kurzweiltech.com/aboutray.html; accessed May 14, 2104.

17 Kurzweil, *The Age of Spiritual Machines*, 174–175.

Raymond Kurzweil (b. 1948), prolific inventor, author, humanitarian and computer scientist, is one of the world's preeminent transhumanists.

Photo © Roland Dobbins (May 2006)

possessed extraordinary versatility for professional musicians but lacked the richness and clarity of sound of the classical instruments. He mused, "Wouldn't it be great if we could use the extraordinary flexible computer-control methods on the beautiful sounds of acoustic instruments?"[18]

Two years later, Kurzweil Music Systems with the assistance of Stevie Wonder produced the Kurzweil 250 which was "the first electronic musical instrument to successfully emulate the complex sound response of a grand piano and virtually all other orchestral instruments."[19]

Between 1964 and 2006, Kurzweil created sixteen new inventions. In 2006, it was the first pocket-sized print-to-speech reading machine for the blind. Touted as "the rightful heir of Thomas Edison," this inventor and entrepreneur extraordinaire was presented the National Medal of Technology, the nation's highest honour in technology, by President Bill Clinton (b. 1946) in 1999. Three years later, he was inducted into the National Inventors Hall of Fame. As the recipient of twenty honorary doctorates and the author of seven books, Dr. Kurzweil has gained well-deserved recognition within the academic world.[20]

In 2007, the National Federation of the Blind presented The Newell Perry Award to Kurzweil, a *bona fide* humanitarian. Dr. Marc Maurer, then-president of the National Federation for the Blind, noted in his presentation speech: "Ray Kurzweil has done more than simply invent revolutionary reading technology; he has helped the blind of America to realize a dream of complete independence."[21]

After writing his newest book in 2012, *How to Create a Mind: The Secret of Human Thought Revealed*, Kurzweil wanted to establish a company where he could devote his time and energy to

---

18 Kurzweil, *The Age of Spiritual Machines*, 176.

19 Kurzweil, *The Age of Spiritual Machines*, 176.

20 "A Brief Career Summary of Ray Kurzweil," (2014); http://www.kurzweiltech.com/ aboutray.html; accessed May 14, 2104.

21 National Federation of the Blind, "Famed Inventor Developed Reading Technology for the Blind," (2007); https://nfb.org/node/1060; accessed June 2, 2014.

create an artificial brain. Our present biological brain, he estimates, has 300 million pattern recognizers in the neocortex, responsible for sensory perception, movement, rational thought and language—"basically, what we regard as 'thinking.'"[22]

In the future when the neocortex is totally digitized, its capacity could be augmented, particularly if it was linked to the Cloud.[23] At that time, people would be able "to use billions and trillions of pattern recognizers, basically whatever we need, and whatever the law of acclerating returns can provide at each point in time."[24]

Knowing that Kurzweil wanted to set up his own company to create an artificial mind, Larry Page, CEO of Google, offered him all the resources of Google to accomplish this feat if he would join their organization as director of engineering. Kurzweil did, in December 2012.

In an interview with *SingularityHUB*, the celebrated futurist revealed he "will work on AI, and one imagines that may include an attempt to reverse engineer the brain."[25] Since the human genome was mapped in 2003, there is only one frontier of human biology left to map: the brain. Within this area of understanding human intelligence, Kurzweil desires to create a computer that has the capability of understanding the variety of nuances in patterns of speech.

On January 10, 2014, Rebecca Costa (b. 1955), author and noted radio host of "The Costa Report," interviewed Kurzweil who at

---

22 Ray Kurzweil, *How to Create a Mind: The Secret of Human Thought Revealed* (New York: Viking, 2012), 35.

23 Cloud computing has become very popular. It encompasses any subscription-based or pay-per-use service which allows computer users to access a variety of "providers large and small delivering a slew of cloud-based services, from full-blown applications to storage services to spam filters." Eric Knorr and Galen Gruman, "What Cloud Computing Really Means," *InfoWorld*; http://www.infoworld.com/d/cloud-computing/what-cloud-computing-really-means-031; accessed May 14, 2014.

24 Kurzweil, *How to Create a Mind*, 123.

25 Jason Dorrier, "Ray Kurzweil Teams Up with Google to Tackle Artificial Intelligence," *SingularityHUB* (December 16, 2012); http://singularityhub.com/2012/12/16/ray-kurzweil-teams-up-with-google-to-tackle-artificial-intelligence/; accessed May 14, 2014.

that time had been employed by Google for just over one year.[26] She asked him to give her an update on his progress in mapping the brain. This eminent inventor admitted that such an undertaking was highly complex and diverse, and it could be accomplished only through the cooperative effort of a very highly skilled team of scientists. But, in spite of these challenges, he was extremely optimistic that great strides were being made. Furthermore, he stated:

> I have a consistent date of 2029. And that does not just mean logical intelligence. It means emotional intelligence: being funny, getting a joke.... That's actually the most complex thing we do. That is what separates computers and humans today. I believe that gap will close by 2029.[27]

Rebecca Costa then commented that in 2013 Google had purchased Boston Dynamics, the world leader in robotic technology. Since Kurzweil had personally started numerous companies, she wanted his opinion concerning this business venture. Without hesitation, he responded that he felt it was a shrewd move. Google, being in the forefront of processing and organizing information through search engines, has also become known for its work on the self-driving car. Google car's record was stellar in that it had covered 804,672 km (500,000 miles) with no accidents—an enviable record by anyone's standard. Thus, it would only seem logical that Google should become involved in the ever-expanding relationship between robotics and artificial intelligence.

In the final segment of the interview, Rebecca Costa noted that Kurzweil had a 94% (102 out of 108) prediction rate. She asked him to indicate what he felt would be the most significant development in the future. The biotech seer stated:

---

26 Rebecca Costa, "Ray Kurzweil Interview," *The Costa Report* (January 10, 2014); http://www.youtube.com/watch?v=_RwXUAjqoCU; accessed May 14, 2014.

27 Steven Levy, "How Ray Kurzweil Will Help Google Make the Ultimate AI Brain," *Wired* (April 25, 2013); http://www.wired.com/business/2013/04/kurzweil-google-ai/; accessed May 14, 2014.

I think we will gain over the next decade more and more mastery over the informational processes underlying biology. We will be able to reprogram our biology, the same way we reprogram our cell phones, away from diseases and aging, and that will be quite dramatic over the next twenty years.[28]

CHANCELLOR OF THE SINGULARITY UNIVERSITY

Singularity University (SU) was the brainchild of Peter Diamandis (b. 1961), physician and noted entrepreneur. The inspiration for this venture came about after reading *The Singularity is Near*. Soon after, Dr. Diamandis successfully enlisted Ray Kurzweil, the author of the book, to join him in creating this unique educational institution. Its mission statement is:

> ...to assemble, educate and inspire leaders who strive to understand and facilitate the development of exponentially advancing technologies in order to address humanity's grand challenges. With the support of a broad range of leaders in academia, business and government, Singularity University hopes to stimulate groundbreaking, disruptive thinking and *solutions aimed at solving some of the planet's most pressing challenges.*[29]

Dr. Kurzweil was appointed the university's first chancellor. As the official head of SU, he has two important tasks. First, he regularly teaches a course, "Future Studies and Forecasting," throughout the year. Second, having become a much sought-after speaker, he, as an ambassador of Singularity University, is able to promote the institution worldwide.

---

28 Costa, "Ray Kurzweil Interview."

29 Peter Diamandis, "Singularity University," (2013); http://www.diamandis.com-about-singularity/; accessed May 14, 2014. Author's italics.

The university's initial financial support of $250,000 came from Larry Page, co-founder of Google.[30] Other corporations joined in, such as Nokia, the Kauffman Foundation and Genentech, to name just a few. NASA's Ames Research Center in California's Silicon Valley was chosen to be the university's campus.

In the summer of 2009, forty students were accepted into a ten-week graduate studies program, with tuition fees at approximately $30,000. The following year, they decided to increase the number of spots available to eighty and received 1,200 applicants.

The course is divided into two five-week segments. During the first five weeks, the students are exposed to 300 hours of formal lectures in ten core academic tracks. Each of these tracks is chaired by a highly qualified instructor. Entrepreneurship, nanotechnology, artificial intelligence, robotics and cognitive computing are some of the areas of study.

PBS reporter, Paul Solman, was given the assignment of examining the nature and purposes of Singularity University. His report stated: "Singularity's mission was to solve humanity's most pressing problems by spurring on new technologies in food, water and energy supposedly scarce but with the tinkering of technology, says Peter Diamandis, potentially abundant."[31]

The last five weeks of the course are devoted to developing entrepreneurial innovations which could alleviate one of the global challenges facing our world. Having divided themselves into groups, students, through brainstorming and dialoguing, have to decide what world condition they will address. Using their entrepreneurial skills, they then adopt a business plan that would establish the necessary strategies to ensure a viable solution and provide sustainable profitability.

Matternet was a business venture initiated by a group of students in the summer of 2011. In underdeveloped countries, small rural

---

30 Ashlee Vance, "Merely Human? That's So Yesterday," *The New York Times* (June 12, 2010); http://www.nytimes.com/2010/06/13/business/13sing.html?pagewanted=all&_r=0; accessed May 14, 2014.

31 Paul Solmon, "Making Sense of Financial News: Abundance," *PBS NewsHour* (April 20, 2012); http://www.singularityweblog.com/pbs-newshour-covers-singularity-university/; accessed May 14, 2014.

businesses have limited access to larger outside markets because of poor roads. This group's solution was to create an aerial vehicle— somewhat like a drone—which could be used to transport goods to nearby commercial centres. Having developed an operational prototype, these students are convinced that the drone, now used primarily for military purposes, has the possibility of being used for peaceful means. Before the course was completed, a company website was built to garner both technical and financial support.

In commenting on the latter half of the course, Chancellor Kurzweil made this pertinent comment: "We teach that the power of entrepreneurship is the best way to learn to do things and to change the world."[32]

That same summer, Nikola Danaylov, the Canadian creator of the *Singularity Weblog*, attended Singularity University. During an interview at his home, he mentioned that SU afforded him the privilege of meeting people from thirty-six different countries. "The whole purpose was to bring these people together from across the globe and live together for ten weeks in order to create a community."[33] As one who works full time in the Singularity movement as a podcaster, Danaylov realized that this was an exceptional opportunity. Not only did he study and socialize with his fellow students—many of whom were leaders in the transhumanist community— but later they were delighted to be interviewed by him. Danaylov's website provides a wealth of information regarding transhumanism.

NANOBOTS AND IMMORTALITY

Death is supposed to be a finality but it is a loss of everyone that you care about.... It's such a profoundly sad, lonely

---

32 Dean Takahashi, "Singularity University Graduates a Class of Tech World Changers," *Venture Beat* (August 28, 2011); http://venturebeat.com/2011/08/28/singularity-university-graduates-a-class-of-tech-world-changers/; accessed May 14, 2014.

33 Interview conducted by the author on Monday, February 18, 2013, in Etobicoke, Ontario, Canada.

feeling that I really can't bear it. So I go back to thinking about *how I'm not going to die.*[34]

These opening words by Ray Kurzweil in the documentary, *Transcendent Man: The Life and Ideas of Ray Kurzweil*, set forth his theme of the conquest of death and the acquisition of personal immortality. Death, a dastardly disease, has had total mastery over our frail biological bodies in the past, but Kurzweil predicts that, in the not too distant future, this domination can finally be ended. Advancing technology will provide the means for individuals to go beyond their natural limitations and to transcend into posthumanity.

In 2009, Kurzweil and Dr. Terry Grossman (b. 1943) co-authored *Transcend: Nine Steps to Living Well Forever*. Its goal was to provide both information and skillsets so that individuals could enhance their personal wellness and also reduce the prospects of aging. The basic underlying assumption is that medicine, namely the study of health, is based on information technology. According to Kurzweil's law of accelerating returns, "the ability to understand, model, stimulate and reprogram the information processes underlying disease and aging will be a thousand times more powerful in 1 decade and a million times more powerful in 2 decades."[35]

As a futurist, Kurzweil has predicted that, by 2045, information technology will become so advanced that the most dramatic moment in modern history—dubbed as the Singularity—will occur. This Singularity can be defined as "the merging of our biological thinking and existence with our technology, resulting *in a world that is still human* but transcends our biological roots."[36]

In time, there will be no difference between humans and machines. The universe would lay unexplored before these posthumans so that they could saturate it with this hybrid intelligence. The capacity of these newly created minds would be trillions upon trillions more powerful than our present ones.

---

34 *Transcendent Man* (2009). Author's italics.

35 Kurzweil and Grossman, *Transcend: Nine Steps to Living Well Forever*, xvii.

36 Kurzweil, *The Singularity is Near*, 9. Author's italics.

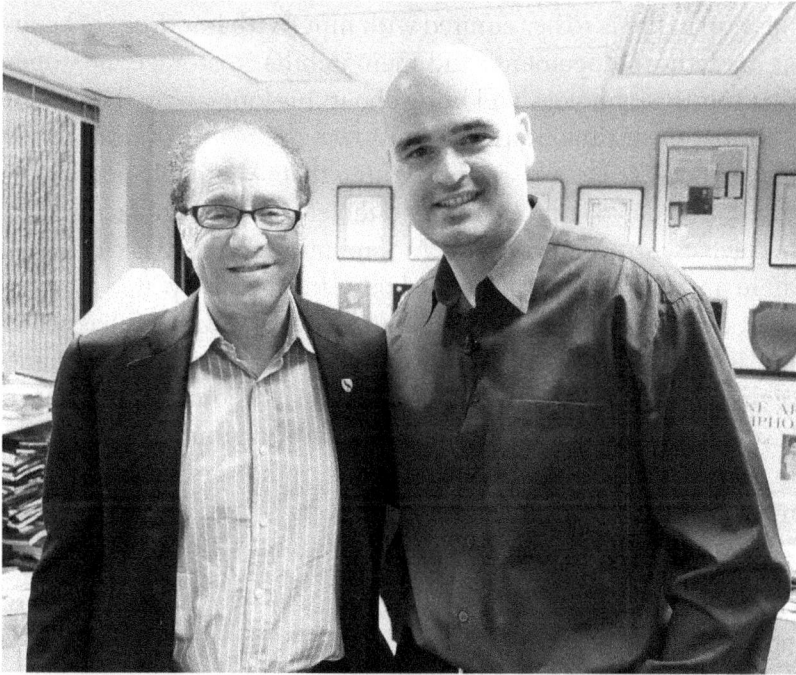

Ray Kurzweil with Nikola Danaylov, in Kurzweil's office, after being interviewed for Danaylov's *Singularity Weblog*. Used with permission.

To maintain these posthuman bodies beyond the Singularity, this pioneer in artificial intelligence envisions that nanotechnology holds the greatest promise. A million nanobots, smaller than a red blood cell, will be infused into a person's blood stream. These miniaturized computers will have the capacity "to perform various services, such as removing toxins, sweeping out debris, correcting DNA errors, repairing and restoring cell membranes... and a myriad of other tasks."[37] Eureka! Technology has finally afforded humanity its greatest dream—immortality.

In the film, *Transcendent Man*, a lachrymose or tearful moment occurred when Ray was standing in front of his father's gravestone. He desperately misses his father who died in 1970 at the age of fifty-eight when Ray was only twenty-two. His greatest

---

37 Kurzweil, *The Singularity is Near*, 256–257.

mission in life is to be reunited with him. With hundreds of boxes of his father's documents and memorabilia in storage, he hopes that future technology will bring about this long-awaited reunion.

In the meantime, Kurzweil must face the reality of death as he just turned 66. He is doing everything that is humanly possible to evade that day. He takes over 150 tablets daily (manufactured by his own company). Every couple of months, his blood is cleansed— "all in an effort to reprogram the body's biochemistry."[38]

In the event that he is overtaken by death, Kurzweil has set in motion an alternative plan—cryonics. He has already made arrangements with the Alcor Life Extension Foundation to have his body cryopreserved. To be buried in the ground or to be cremated is unthinkable. Even though we do not presently have the means of reviving bodies cryonically preserved, technology, as always will be the *panacea* to gain eternal life—and thus we "will be like God."[39]

38 Michael Shermer, "The Immortalist: A Review of *Transcendent Man: A Film About the Life and Ideas of Ray Kurzweil*," *The Work of Michael Shermer* (2009); http://www.michaelshermer.com/tag/ray-kurzweil/; accessed May 14, 2014.

39 Genesis 3:4.

07

AUBREY DE GREY
The war on aging

BECOMING A RENOWNED BIOLOGIST

"Justify your existence!"[1] These words abruptly brought Adelaide Carpenter into the world of Aubrey de Grey, host of a birthday party for a Cambridge graduate student. Since he had to attend to some electrical problem and hurried away, she was not able to respond to his terse remark. But, in the months to follow, she would have ample opportunity to come to know and become romantically attached to this most intriguing Englishman. Though she was nineteen years his senior, they were married in April 1991.

Dr. Carpenter, "a highly accomplished American geneticist and an expert microscopist," had been on a sabbatical leave from the University of California in San Diego.[2] After her marriage to

---

1 Jonathan Weiner, *Long for This World: The Strange Science of Immortality* (New York: HarperCollins, 2011), 47.

2 Sherwin Nuland, "Do You Want to Live Forever?" *MIT Technology Review* (February 1, 2005); section 2:2; http://www.technologyreview.com/featuredstory/403654/do-you-want-to-live-forever/; accessed May 14, 2014.

Aubrey, she accepted a position in the genetics department at Cambridge University. Aubrey, on the other hand, worked in the private sector as a software engineer after graduating in computer science from the same institution. Through his wife, Adelaide, he learned that the genetics department at Cambridge needed a software specialist to run a database on fruit fly research. He was hired in 1992 and held that post until 2006.

Being married to a renowned biologist was indeed a boon for Aubrey. During their innumerable dinner conversations, his wife piqued his interest in the study of biology. In time, Aubrey broached the topic of human longevity. Gerontology, the study of aging, was never a topic that interested Adelaide, but Aubrey, on the other hand, became impassioned with this most universal and dreaded malady; he quipped that "he loved a problem with the reputation for impossibility."[3] Life is viewed differently depending on one's vantage point; in the early stages, life breathes with vitality and hope, but as it draws to a close, life becomes marked with frailty and even despair.

Aubrey De Grey persisted; he spent hours pouring over biological texts and scientific journals and became a recognized authority on human aging. Thus, "a part-time passion for biology turned into a full time crusade" against senescence.[4] In 1999, he published a highly technical book, *The Mitochondrial Free Radical Theory of Aging*. In recognition for his significant contribution in the field of aging, Cambridge University granted him a Ph.D. in biology even though he only had an undergraduate degree in computer science from the university. To the world at large, de Grey had become "more than a man; he was a movement."[5]

---

3   Weiner, *Long for This World*, 48.

4   Channel 4 documentary, *Do You Want to Live Forever?* Producer and director Christopher Sykes (2006); http://www.youtube.com/watch?v=JtHgIJ6kalk; accessed May 14, 2014.

5   Nuland, "Do You Want to Live Forever?" section 2:3.

DEVELOPING AN INTERNATIONAL PERSONA

The word "iconoclast" comes from two Greek words: *eikon* (image) and *klastēs* (one who breaks or destroys). Thus, an iconoclast is a person who breaks or delights in challenging conventional beliefs or standards. Such is Aubrey David Nicholas Jasper de Grey who was born in London, England, in 1963.

His extraordinary name reveals much about his mother, Cordelia, an iconoclast in her own right. One author referred to her as a "bohemian artist."[6] Nevertheless, as a single parent, she raised her son, Aubrey, who never met his father but he lavished much praise upon his mother for giving him "an enormous really strong desire to learn—a desire to understand the world...a strong desire to understand myself."[7]

Recognizing that her son was gifted intellectually, she wanted him to have a good education. To that end, she sent young Aubrey to Sussex House, an independent boys' school, with students ranging in age from eight to thirteen.

The motto of Sussex House was taken from Psalm 61:2 "Lead me to the rock that is higher than I." The school's prospectus states: "The spiritual life of the school is an important, enriching element. All boys study Religious Education, attend Assemblies which include prayers.... The religious ethos of the school is Anglican."[8] A note of interest is that Aubrey de Grey is listed as one of the writers of the alumni magazine, *The Old Cadogan*.

Upon graduation from Sussex House, Aubrey went on to the prestigious private boys' school—Harrow. Unlike Sussex House which dates back to 1952, Harrow was established in 1572. The alumni includes such illustrious people as the poet Lord Byron (1788–1824) and former British Prime Minister Sir Winston Churchill (1874–1965).

---

6 Weiner, *Long for This World*, 16.

7 "Big Think Interview with Aubrey de Grey," *Big Think* (October 21, 2009); http://bigthink.com/videos/big-think-interview-with-aubrey-de-grey; accessed May 14, 2014.

8 "Sussex House" (2009); http://www.sussexhouseschool.co.uk/main_pages/spiritualLife.html; accessed May 14, 2014.

These private boys' schools provided Aubrey with a first-rate academic education. Both schools, demonstrating a mark of distinction, enforced a very strict dress code, especially Harrow with its suits and straw hats. Possibly while a university student at Cambridge or thereafter—in total variance to his many years of private schooling—the latent persona of Aubrey David Nicholas Jasper de Grey emerged. Standing 1.82 metres (6 feet) tall, Aubrey sports his most iconoclastic trademark—a chestnut Rasputin-like beard that extends down over his chest.

Sherwin Nuland (1930–2014), noted professor of clinical surgery at Yale University and author of *How We Die: Reflections on Life's Final Chapter* (1994), wrote this account of his first meeting with Aubrey de Grey. "He was dressed like an unkempt graduate student, uncaring of tailoring considerations of any sort, wearing a hip-length black mackinaw-type coat that was borderline shabby. ... I saw that de Grey's long straight hair was held in a ponytail by a circular band of bright red wool."[9]

Dr. Nuland made mention that de Grey daily consumed numerous pints of beer. Since he only weighs 66 kg (147 lb), everyone who is aquainted with him is amazed that being an inveterate drinker has not affected his weight.

While a student at Cambridge, Aubrey purchased his first punt, a flat-bottomed boat with a square-cut bow. Since then, he has become an avid punter. Both he and his wife spend many of their leisure hours punting. In many ways, Adelaide is a perfect complement to her husband. She possesses the same uncaring attitude toward attire and is as totally focused on research as her soul mate. They have been married for twenty-two years and have no desire to raise children.

Aubrey's mother believed that religious training was important for her son. On a regular basis, he was sent to the Anglican church. There can be no doubt that the religious stance taken by Sussex House pleased her. It was while Aubrey was a student at Harrow that he took his confirmation classes. Later, he viewed such a

---

9   Nuland, "Do You Want to Live Forever?" section 4:1.

ritual as having no spiritual significance upon his life.[10] When, at the age of forty-six, he was reminiscing about his religious life as a teenager, he recalled:

> ...with regard to my views about whether God exists; you know, whether I should be religious or not. On that really my decision was not to make a decision, so way back in my teens...how would I behave differently if I were religious versus if I were not religious, and I realized that there was no difference at all; that I already had decided that what I wanted to do with my life was to benefit humanity.... *So, I guess the best way to describe my own view is I am agnostic.*[11]

Around the age of eight or nine, his mother insisted that her son should take piano lessons. This precocious youngster refused; he reasoned that there were enough pianists in the world; so, why would he want to invest his time in pursuing such an endeavour? The study of science was an area in which he felt that he could make a difference in this world. Even at that young age, he recognized the positive effects on prioritizing one's efforts.

Dr. de Grey has been heralded as the foremost scholar in the field of theoretical biogerontology.[12] His passion against aging has been fueled by the realization that, worldwide, 150,000 people die daily; 100,000 or two-thirds of these deaths are from natural causes. Such horrendous statistics have been the catalyst that spurred him into action. Historian David Boyd Haycock has captured De Grey's impact: "Intelligent, perceptive, witty and personable, de Grey has helped place biogerontology firmly on the public map."[13]

---

10 Weiner, *Long for This World*, 214.

11 "Big Think Interview with Aubrey de Grey." Author's italics.

12 Nuland, "Do You Want to Live Forever?" section 2:2.

13 David Boyd Haycock, *Mortal Coil: A Short History of Living Longer* (New Haven: Yale University Press, 2008), 206.

SENS: A PROACTIVE ATTACK ON AGING

On June 25, 2000, Dr. de Grey experienced his "eureka" moment at the Marriott Hotel in Manhattan Beach, California. The day before, he had spent many fruitless hours at an anti-aging conference. Tired and frustrated, he had a restless night, but at four o'clock in the morning, this alarming revelation occurred to him: "Aging is not something inherently mysterious, beyond our power to fathom. There is no ticking time bomb—just the accumulation of damage."[14]

Later, in a lecture at the Singularity University, de Grey illustrated diagrammatically his revolutionary ideology against senescence:[15]

Metabolism $\longrightarrow$ Damage $\longrightarrow$ Pathology

The logic of this approach—based on the assumption that aging is a disease—is compelling. To eliminate the damage caused by metabolism at the molecular and cellular level, this anti-aging guru has enumerated "seven deadly things" that are responsible for the aging process.[16] Having a penchant for acronyms, he devised a program known as SENS (Strategies for Engineered Negligible Senescence).

To illustrate the foundational truth behind SENS, de Grey has put forth this cogent analogy. There are vintage cars which are over a hundred years old and are still in good running condition. How could that be? It was achieved only through constant maintenance by its owner. Similarly, de Grey reasons, such is the case with the human body, which also is a machine—"a great deal more complicated than any man-made machine"[17]—but

---

14 Aubrey de Grey, *Ending Aging: The Rejuvenation Breakthroughs That Could Reverse Human Aging in Our Lifetime* (New York: St. Martin's, 2008), 21.

15 "Aubrey de Grey–In Pursuit of Longevity" (2009), Singularity University; http://www.youtube.com/watch?v=HTMNfU7zftQ; accessed May 14, 2014. See also de Grey's, *Ending Aging*, 42.

16 Consult de Grey's *Ending Aging*, 43. Both the damage and the possible means of rectifying each are listed.

17 De Grey, *Ending Aging*, 22.

Aubrey de Grey (b. 1963) leads the crusade against the effects of aging on the human body. He is Chief Science Officer of the SENS Research Foundation, which is engaged in research to find cures for the diseases of aging.

nevertheless, it also needs to be thoroughly maintained.

A prolific author, Dr. de Grey used his pen to publicize his war on aging by writing *Ending Aging: The Rejuvenation Breakthroughs That Could Reverse Human Aging in Our Lifetime* (2007). This book outlines the seven deadly things and has become "a road-map aimed at defeating aging."[18] To further this revolutionary approach for body rejuvenation, de Grey established the SENS Research Foundation and became its Chief Science Officer in 2009.

The Foundation's research "emphasizes the application of re-generative medicine to age-related disease, with the intent of re-pairing underlying damage to the body's tissues, cells, and mole-cules. [It's] goal is to help build the industry that will cure the diseases of aging."[19] The facility is located in Mountain View, California, where researchers, covering all the scientific fields of aging, have been brought together, and according to de Grey, they are making headway in their assault against senescence.

Awareness and education are extremely important components in informing the general public of the aims and goals of the SENS Research Foundation. Having at least fifty speaking engagements worldwide each year, de Grey uses this forum to make the work of the Foundation known. But the ultimate success of this life exten-sion program rests upon the financial support that the SENS leadership must garner in order to keep the project viable.

Dr. de Grey has stressed repeatedly that the goal is the mainte-nance of healthy bodies, not longevity. Aging is not considered to be a natural or normal state of life. Medical intervention is the only means that can "maintain and restore the structure of the human body at the molecular, cellular and organ level *as it is in young adulthood.*"[20]

---

18 "Top 10 Singularitarians of All Time," *Singularity Weblog* (January 23, 2010); http://www.singularityweblog.com/top-10-singularitarians; accessed May 14, 2014.

19 Sens Research Foundation, "About SENS Research Foundation" (2014); http://www.sens.org/about/about-the-foundation; accessed May 14, 2014.

20 "Health, Longevity and Regenerative Medicine with Dr. Aubrey de Grey," (August 3, 2012); interviewed by Phil Micans; http://www.youtube.com/watch?v=sbC3_kOclxI; accessed May 14, 2014. Author's italics.

ENZYMES AND AGING

After the rise of Darwinism, the perennial problem of aging and death has been viewed within a totally new framework. Since the primary role of evolutionary development was to bring forth the diversity of life, why then is there death? The mere fact that death even exists within a life-creating system seems very contradictory. Some evolutionists have speculated that natural selection initiated death in order to eliminate the unfit—the weak and sickly— which would hinder upward progress. To others, "aging is not an aspiration; aging is just an accident. Death is not made by Darwin's process; it arises because there are places where Darwin's process is powerless to go."[21]

A committed evolutionist, Aubrey de Grey began to ponder this question: How do evolutionary forces rid the environment of unwanted contaminants? How could this process of cleaning up the earth be related to aging? Known as an original thinker who looks beyond the traditional box of gerontology, this crusader for life had a flash of genius while on a visit to Dresden, Germany.

If the enzymes of the bacteria within the soil which were responsible for decomposition could be located, could they not be placed within the body to eradicate the accumulated "cellular garbage"? But where would be the best place to find these bacteria? On a British television program, he explained:

I realized that bacteria should exist that would have the technology—that is have the enzymes to break down these substances [cellular garbage]. All we have to do is find these bacteria and get the enzymes into our bodies. The right place to look may well be *a graveyard!*[22]

As a frequent guest speaker at Singularity University, de Grey is very supportive of transhumanism. The obvious question is: How does his theory of rejuvenational health relate to transhumanism?

---

21 Weiner, *Long for This World*, 213.
22 Channel 4 documentary, *Do You Want to Live Forever?* Italics added.

He does not personally believe that technology and humanity will merge together within the foreseeable future. Instead he envisions "the creation of friendly general artificial intelligences, namely robots or other completely external devices which would make our lives safe" and will provide the necessary protection that will allow people to live longer.[23]

In the event of a premature death, de Grey has a contingency plan. He wants his head severed from his body and frozen in liquid nitrogen. Such a procedure can be carried out at the Alcor Life Extension Foundation in Scottsdale, Arizona.

Hope of extending life indefinitely beams from the conclusion of *Ending Aging* when Aubrey de Grey confidently states: "I shall look forward to shaking your hand in a future where engineered negligible senescence is a reality: where we can enjoy dramatically extended lives in a new summer of vigor and health."[24]

---

23 Aubrey de Grey interviewed by Nikola Danaylov on *Singularity 1 on 1*; "Longevity Escape Velocity May Be Closer Than We Think" (2011); http://www.singularityweblog.com/aubrey-de-greys-singularity-podcast-longevity-escape-velocity-maybe-closer-than-we-think/; accessed May 14, 2014.

24 De Grey, *Ending Aging*, 338.

08

KEVIN WARWICK
Becoming a cyborg

A HUMAN REMOTE CONTROL

"**B**ored of being human? Limited in what you can do? Brain doesn't perform how it should? What are the possibilities of an upgrade?"[1] were questions posed by Kevin Warwick (b. 1954) at the beginning of his presentation at TEDx Warwick in 2012.[2] Providing meaningful answers to these questions has become both the focus and passion of his life's work.

A British engineer, Professor Warwick received his Ph.D. in 1982 from Imperial College, London. Dr. Warwick was professor of cybernetics at England's Reading University for twenty-five years (until June 2014), where he was involved in studying two specific areas: first, the interface between computers and the

---

1 TEDx Warwick, "Kevin Warwick—Implants & Technology: The Future of Healthcare?" (March 22, 2012); http://youtu.be/Z8HeFNJjujo; accessed June 2, 2014.

2 TED is an aconym for "Technology, Entertainment, Design." Established in 1984 as a one-time conference, it is now held annually. Speakers are invited to present the most current ideas in the fields of science and culture. Its motto is, "Ideas worth spreading."

human nervous system and, second, robotics. Through his research, he has gained international renown. He has received numerous awards, including seven honorary doctorates. Warwick is
presently deputy vice-chancellor at Coventry University and a
visiting professor at Reading.

A prodigious author,[3] Warwick has continually maintained
that, "Just as we humans split from our chimpanzee cousins, so
cyborgs [cybernetic organisms] will split from humans."[4] In 1997,
in his book, *March of the Machines: Why the New Race of Robots
Will Rule the World*, he prophesied that by 2050 the world would
be dominated by robots.[5] He concluded by stating:

> We have the technology, we have the ability, I believe, to
> create machines that will not only be as intelligent as
> humans but that will go on to be far more intelligent
> still.... There will be no way to stop the march of the
> machines.[6]

Warwick stepped onto the world's stage in August 1998, when
a Radio Frequency Identification Device (RFID), a tiny glass con-
tainer full of transponders, was implanted beneath the skin of his
left forearm. His laboratory was so wired that "when he walked
through doorways, the lights would turn on; when he walked into
his study, his computer would boot up."[7] For a month, Professor
Warwick was, in essence, a "human remote control."

The insertion of the RFID came with certain risks. In a recent
interview, Warwick mentioned that "the doctor cut away from
the nervous system the mylan sheath and if infection got in, he

---

3   See http://centaur.reading.ac.uk/view/creators/90000341.html; accessed June 2,
2014. The number of publications listed for Professor Warwick was 373.

4   Kevin Warwick, *I, Cyborg* (London: Century, 2002), 4.

5   See Ray Kurzweil's prediction of 2045 on page 96.

6   Kevin Warwick, *March of the Machines: Why the New Race of Robots Will Rule the
World* (London: Century, 1997), 257.

7   Ben Goertzel, *The Path to Posthumanity* (Bethesda: Academica Press, 2006), 235.

Kevin Warwick (b. 1954) was the first human to have an RFID implanted underneath his skin. Since then, Professor Warwick has performed all kinds of experiments related to technology and sensory apprehension and robotics. He believes that by 2050 the world will be dominated by robots. © Andy Miah/Flikr/Creative Commons

could lose the use of his left hand."[8] Thankfully, he experienced no infection or body rejection.

In 2013, some fifteen years later, the RFID—first used by Kevin Warwick—has become commonplace; it is used as an anti-theft device in most stores. In my apartment building, this same technology is used to gain entry into all the restricted areas.

Presently, some of Warwick's graduate students are performing experiments in which magnets are surgically inserted into their fingertips. In turn, they are connected to ultrasonic sensors on their heads. Through the vibrations of the magnets, these students can "feel" the proximity of objects. Thus, the magnets have become a sensory substitution.[9]

"CAPTAIN CYBORG"

In March 2002, Professor Warwick embarked on a more dangerous venture. He had an internal Utah array—3mm by 3mm—containing 100 electrodes placed within his arm; each electrode was 1.5 mm long and was connected directly to his nervous system. To provide additional electronic support for the array, a cuff was placed around his forearm.

"The goal was to fire electrical impulses into his brain to see whether a human could learn to sense, interpret and reply to computer-generated stimuli."[10] Since this medical procedure had never been done before, there was the possibility of nerve damage, infection or, even worse, severe brain injury. The evening prior to surgery, in order to alleviate his apprehension, the future cyborg read Jean-Paul Sartre's *The Age of Reason*.[11] His choice of literature speaks volumes concerning his atheistic religious persuasion.

---

8   Kevin Warwick interviewed by Nikola Danaylov on *Singularity 1 on 1*; "Be/Come the Cy/Borg" (2011); http://www.singularityweblog.com/?s=Kevin+Warwick; accessed June 2, 2014.

9   TEDxWarwick, "Kevin Warwick."

10 Eben Harrell, "My Body, My Laboratory," *Time* (March 6, 2011); http://www.time.com/time/magazine/article/0,9171,2050030,00.html; accessed June 2, 2014.

11 Warwick, *I, Cyborg*, 205.

"Captain Cyborg" (aka Professor Warwick) after an internal Utah array was implanted in his arm. He was able to make a mechanical hand mimic his own hand movements.

The two-hour operation was successful; the preoperative fears never materialized. One experiment that captivated the imagination of the media was his ability to make a mechanical hand that he had constructed mimic his own hand movements. For the first time, a human could control a mechanical device through his own body.

Buoyed by this success, Warwick travelled from England to Columbia University in New York. Here, a continent away, he was able to control the same robotic hand via the Internet just as if he had been in the same room.

Publicity mounted when his wife, Irena, had an array placed in her arm. Blindfolded, Irena was to indicate when Kevin moved his fingers. At first, she felt nothing. The power was increased. Then, she exclaimed, "I felt it." Kevin moved his fingers at differ-ent intervals, and each time Irena felt the sensation. They had successfully demonstrated that it was possible to send signals through the computer from one person to another.[12]

During an interview in 2010, nearly a decade later, Professor Warwick went on record that he is prepared to enter into a more perilous and even further uncharted "cyborg" territory. This time, he would like to have a powerful chip inserted into his brain. He made this remark:

> At the age of sixty, I am ready to take the risk. I have done a lot of things.... You only have one life and I believe that this is something we can do and we have the technology about now to link a human brain to a computer network.... *I do not want to die without having tried it.*[13]

It is no wonder that he has been dubbed, "Captain Cyborg."

DEEP BRAIN STIMULATION

As a transhumanist, Warwick is not only a futurist but also a caring and compassionate humanist. Since 2006, Dr. Warwick has been involved in bringing relief to those who are suffering from Parkinson's disease. He has been working with University of Oxford neurosurgeon, Tipu Aziz (b. 1966), in Deep Brain Stimulation (DBS). While a patient is conscious, a 7-cm probe is placed within their brain which, in turn, is connected by wires to a type of pacemaker device (called an impulse generator, or IPG).

The remarkable results of DBS can be seen most dramatically in the life of Michael Robins. He had been suffering from Parkinson's disease for eight years. It was only a short time after a team of surgeons completed the surgery that the retired British naval engineer realized that, for the first time in eight years, his limbs were not shaking.

---

12 Warwick, *I, Cyborg*, 285.

13 Kevin Warwick interviewed by Nikola Danaylov on *Singularity 1 on 1*; "You Have to Take Risks to Be Part of the Future" (2010); http://www.singularityweblog.com/kevin-warwick-on-singularity-podcast-you-have-to-take-risks-to-be-part-of-the-future/; accesed June 2, 2014. Author's italics.

"Thanks to pioneering surgery, the debilitating effects of Parkinson's disease that were wrecking his life were now under tight control."[14] One can watch a video demonstration and see why Robins speaks so highly of this medical procedure. He turns off his IPG (a battery-powered neurostimulator) and immediately the violent tremors recur. Then, by activating his IPG device, they subside and Robins returns to normal.[15]

Today, 60,000 people who have neurodegenerative diseases are being treated by DBS.[16] Studies seem to suggest that the treatment is still effective after ten years. Certainly, after being diagnosed with this disease, Michael J. Fox (b. 1961), a Canadian actor and author, has become an ardent campaigner in bringing awareness of this serious affliction to the public.

ANIMAT

Another first occurred in 2007. "Not content with upgrading existing brains. Warwick and his team have also tried to grow them."[17] Taking neurons from rats, they place them in a Petri dish and feed them minerals and nutrients. In a short period of time, these biological brains grow and interconnect into a viable but complicated network of neurons.

To operate a small, four-wheeled robot named Animat, these neurons are placed within the control circuit of the robot. Sixty electrodes or sensors emit electrical impulses to the cluster of neurons which, in turn, stimulates them to send their own signals which control the movements of Animat. At first, the neurons' control of the simple-wheeled robot were quite

---

14 Robin McKie, "Hundreds Shouted At Me, Roll Over and Die," *The Guardian* (May 15, 2005); http://www.theguardian.com/science/2005/may/15/medicineandhealth.health; accessed June 2, 2014.

15 "Parkinson's Disease" (May 14, 2009); http://youtu.be/KDjWdtDyz5I; accessed June 2, 2014.

16 Hannah Waters, "Deep Brain Stimulation Hinders Parkinson's for Ten Years and Counting," *Nature Medicine*, Spoonful of Medicine blog (August 8, 2011); http://blogs.nature.com/spoonful/2011/08/deep_brain_stimulation_hinders.html; accessed June 2, 2014.

17 TEDx Warwick, "Kevin Warwick."

erratic but, in time, this rat-robot could be "taught" to follow definite patterns.

From Dr. Warwick's perspective, this Animat technology, has tremendous medical potential. He has stated:

> We have an aging society, particularly in the Western world; so, problems such as Alzheimer's disease, Parkinson's disease, and even strokes are going to be much more prevalent.... What we are doing in this research is trying to understand the basic characteristics within a brain. So, hopefully for some of these diseases at least, we can find ways of remedying them, but maybe even discover a cure.[18]

To inform the general public about the introductory principles concerning transhumanism, or more specifically, artificial intelligence, Professor Warwick has written a book titled, *Artificial Intelligence: The Basics* (2012).

BECOMING A CYBORG

The next momentous event in the world's history—the Singularity—will occur, according to Warwick, around 2050. For the first time, humanity will be in a position to shed its bodies burdened with limitations both physical and intellectual and become something better—cyborgs. For Warwick, this would be the fulfilment of a lifelong dream.

As an agnostic, he sees that God, even if he existed, could not be of any assistance. More tragic is the inevitability of death—something which is even beyond God's control. Rather, it is a dreadful consequence that natural selection has directed against all living things, resulting in the total obliteration of all consciousness and existence.

Cyborgation is the only solution. Without the merging of humans with machines, humanity as a species is doomed to

---

18 "Robot with a Biological Brain" (University of Reading, 2008); http://www.youtube.com/watch?v=wACltn9QpCc; accessed June 2, 2014.

obilivion; in constrast, "Machines can be born over and over, and retain their memories from one life into the next."[19] In the event of any malfunction, a new replacement can be installed. "In this way, machines could become immortal."[20]

But one final query does remain: Since this futurist is nearing sixty years old, what happens to him if he dies before the Singularity arrives? Will he be cryopreserved at the Alcor Life Extension Foundation in Scottsdale, Arizona, with his fellow transhumanists, Ray Kurzweil and Aubrey de Grey?

---

19 Warwick, *March of the Machines*, xi.
20 Warwick, *March of the Machines*, xi.

09

NATASHA VITA-MORE
Designing a transhuman

FROM ARTIST TO PHILOSOPHER

Natasha Vita-More (b. 1950) was born Nancie Clark in Bronxville, an affluent suburb of Eastchester, New York. Her young, inquisitive mind was influenced by a large and creative family. Even though Natasha attended an Episcopalian Church with her family nearly every Sunday, she began to have reservations about its doctrines and practices—but she still had a deep regard for the church's rituals. Eventually, as a college-aged student, she jettisoned Christianity as being the sole truth and sought out alternatives, such as Unitarian Universalism, Buddhism and spirituality.

Leaving home, Vita-More enrolled in the University of Memphis to study in the art program where she worked with the dean of the art department to design her own artistic program. Her motto has always been that an artist must "experience" life before creating art. Currently, this practice has been adopted by the art departments of many universities where students are required to be involved in off-campus projects.

A requirement for this particular art program was for each student to write a thesis. Natasha chose "Navajo Mysticism in the Fine Arts." To gain firsthand knowledge of their religious beliefs and lore, she arranged to live with the Navajo for a period of time at the Big Mountain reservation in Arizona. In 1974, she graduated with a Bachelor of Fine Arts (Honours) in painting, sculpture and printmaking.

With her degree in fine arts in hand, Vita-More moved to Italy where she was a guest lecturer on performance art at the Accademia di Belle Arti di Ravenna. After gaining more cross-cultural insights, she returned to the United States to live in Telluride, Colorado, where she started her first business, a fine art gallery and graphic design firm. In 1979, the Telluride Science and Technology Festival featured "Arts and Science 79." Being a visual and performance artist, she was invited to be a participant. In her interaction with other artists and scientists, she was thoroughly amazed at how arts and technology were being used to complement one another.

This was in 1979. So, the human computer integration was fairly new in the arts. Harold Cohen [b. 1928] was the first to use artificial intelligence and robots in his work. I met Harold and a number of other highly innovative artists and scientists and my life was changed![1]

To learn more about emerging technologies, Natasha Vita-More moved to Los Angeles. Here, she worked in the film industry as an artist-in-residence for the Los Angeles Film Festival, and also at Francis Ford Coppola's movie studio. She also wrote cover stories for the *Hollywood Reporter* and produced several videos, one of which received special mention at the Women's Video Festival. A woman with energy and purpose, she was drawn to celebrities such as architect and designer Buckminster Fuller (1895–1983),

---

1 Natasha Vita-More interviewed by Nikola Danaylov on *Singularity 1 on 1* (2011); http://www.singularityweblog.com/natasha-vita-more-on-singularity-1-on-1/; accessed June 2, 2014.

psychologist and pioneer in psychedelic therapy Timothy Leary (1920–1996) and stage director Robert Wilson (b. 1941).

But still, within, there was something missing. Answers to the questions of life occupied Natasha's mind: Why are we here? Where are we going? Then, out of the blue, she spotted a picture of a man on the cover of the *Los Angeles Reader*. It was Fereidoun M. Esfandiary, whose writings on the future of humans and the possibility of life extension as a transhuman captivated her.[2] Better known as FM-2030, he had a profound effect on shaping Natasha's insights concerning how humans could be in command of their own evolutionary development. Coupled with her unique sense of life, cross-cultural experiences and the arts, she readily embraced transhumanism.

Combining her passion for the arts and design with filmmaking and evolutionary thought, Vita-More produced her first film, *Breaking Away* (1980), which marked what now can be seen as the beginning of transhumanist arts. Three years later, she and FM-2030 formulated the "Transhumanist Arts Statement." This was the first document that clearly established a philosophical platform, describing the interaction between transhumanist arts and science/technologies.

In 1991, she was at a dinner party at Timothy Leary's house where she met Max More, the author who wrote the first philosophical treatise concerning transhumanism.[3] During their conversation that evening, he explained to Natasha the principles of extropy—the concept that, through human intelligence and technology, humanity can be endowed with capabilities to accomplish anything that it desires.[4]

Shortly thereafter, Natasha invited him to make a guest appearance on her local cable TV show, *TransCentury Update*. For her audience, he was able to demonstrate why extropy was, in essence, foundational to one's understanding of transhumanism.

---

2   See Chapter 5.

3   Max More, "Transhumanism: Toward a Futurist Philosophy" (1990).

4   See Max More interviewed by Adam A. Ford; "The Singularity and Transhumanism" (2011); http://youtu.be/1xIQgBXw9-0; accessed June 2, 2014.

Thus, by means of her interaction with this transhumanist philosopher who later would become her husband, Vita-More was able to apply these extropian concepts to her work in the arts and technology.

Armed with the philosophical insights gained from Max More, she created the "Transhumanist Manifesto" (1994). It reads:

- We are transhumans.
- Transhumans integrate the most eminent progression of creativity and sensibility merged by discovery.
- Transhumans want to elevate and extend life.
- Transhumans seek to expand life.
- As our tools and ideas continue to evolve, so too shall we.
- We are designing the technologies to enhance our senses and increase our understanding.
- The transhumanist ecology and freedom exercises self-awareness and self-responsibility.
- Let us choose to be transhumanist not only in our bodies, but also in our values.
- Toward diversity, multiplicity.
- Toward non-partisan ideology (transpolitics, transpartisan, transmodernity).
- Toward transhuman rights of morphological freedom, existence safety, personhood preservation.
- Toward a more humane transhumanity.[5]

In 1997, this "Transhuman Manifesto" was included with a collection of writings placed on board the *Cassini-Huygens* spacecraft on its mission to Saturn. Someone quipped that if this manifesto was discovered by life on Saturn, the first words that they would read would be: "We are transhumans."

As part of the film industry during the 1980s and early 1990s,

---

5 Natasha Vita More, "Transhumanist Manifesto," *Transhumanist Arts and Culture* (2011); http://www.transhumanist.biz/transhumanmanifesto.htm. *Ed. note: this link is no longer working, and I am unable to find another online source.*

Natasha Vita-More (b. 1950) is a transhumanist philosopher, artist, filmmaker and designer. She formulated the first "Tranhumanist Arts Statement" in 1982 and created the "Tranhumanist Manifesto" in 1994. © Humanity+. Used with permission.

Vita-More was enjoying a lucrative and successful career, but felt a longing for something more. She later commented:

> It has been a continuous journey to find not only the sciences and technologies which could help us develop a future of numerous potentials and solve a lot of problems that we have such as environmental problems.... But I was looking for a set of visionaries who not only understood these [problems] but wanted to be the purveyors of these ideas. So, I feel very fortunate that I did meet a lot of futur-ists and scholars of the human enhancement sciences.[6]

---

6 Vita-More interviewed by Nikola Danaylov on *Singularity 1 on 1* (2011).

In pursuing the philosophical and theoretical dimensions of transhumanism and the arts, Vita-More had to prepare herself for a career change. To attain a sound understanding of science, she enrolled at the University of Houston's program on Future Studies in 2006 and obtained a Master of Science degree.

Natasha still felt that more graduate studies were needed to gain a better understanding of the interaction between technology and the knowledge of human nature. She felt that the University of Plymouth in Britain provided her with the best resources to achieve her goal. So, she entered the university's program and graduated with a Master of Philosophy degree in 2008. Four years later, she received her doctorate from the same institution. Her dissertation was: "Life Expansion: Toward a Theory of Artistic and Design-Based Approaches to the Transhuman/Posthuman" (2012).

What is the state of transhumanism today? Natasha Vita-More and her philosopher-husband, Max More, have co-authored *The Transhumanist Reader: Classical and Contemporary Essays on the Science, Technology, and Philosophy of the Human Future* (2013). Forty leading transhumanists have contributed a variety of essays related to emerging technologies and their relationship to human enhancement.

It is no wonder that Cintra Wilson, a reporter for the *The New York Times*, has correctly deemed this talented woman to be "the first female Transhumanist philosopher."[7]

PRIMO POSTHUMAN

"Denigrating human biology is not the telos of life for transhumanists,"[8] wrote Dr. Vita-More. As a professional artist, she wanted to rectify this misconception by creating "Primo Posthuman," which was redesigned in 2012. Its futuristic body, a finely-tuned machine, is easily recognizable as a human.

---

7 Cintra Wilson, "Droid Rage," *The New York Times* (October 21, 2007); http://www.nytimes.com/2007/10/21/style/tmagazine/21droid.html?_r=0; accessed June 2, 2014.

8 Natasha Vita-More, "The Aesthetics of Transhumanism," *Humanity+* (April 22, 2011); http://hplusmagazine.com/2013/04/19/the-aesthetics-of-transhumanism/; accessed June 3, 2014.

Asked why she chose a human form instead of some animal like a dolphin or a cyborg, Vita-More replied: "Since 'metal' and 'machine' suggest a cold, hard, non-feeling aesthetic, I wanted to introduce a humane characteristic that symbolizes our human strength, perceptibility, intelligence and sensuality."[9] Furthermore, the continuity of identity between human and posthuman would garner greater acceptance among the general populace and also present a more positive and acceptable image of posthumanity.

In an interview some months later, Vita-More clarified her commitment to the protection of one's personhood in what she calls "The Whole Body Prosthetic." There has been a great deal of discussion of backing up the mind but, as Vita-More contends, why not back up the entire body? Her rationale would be:

So, we need to think of the continuity of identity over substrates, over platforms and over time. So what is that continuousness of identity? How can we protect and sustain it? So, what am I looking for in the future? I think that the most consequential aspects of our wanting to enhance and to live longer is ourselves—our mind, our consciousness, our cognition, our intellect, our memories and everything that forms who we are as persons. That is what we need to protect![10]

Utilizing the expected scientific advances in nano/bio technology within the coming decades, she has designed a future body prototype known as Primo Posthuman with a metabrain, having 100 quadrillion synapses as compared to a human's 100 trillion synapses. Its intellectual capacity would far exceed its human counterpart. Placed within its circulatory system, nanobots

---

9 Ben Goertzel, "Ben Goertzel Interviews Natasha Vita-More," *Humanity+* (January 18, 2013): http://hplusmagazine.com/2013/01/18/ben-goertzel-interviews-natasha-vita-more/; accessed June 3, 2014.

10 Natasha Vita-More interviewed by Nikola Danaylov on *Singularity 1 on 1*; "Whole Body Prosthetic" (September 2013); https://www.youtube.com/watch?v=8LucitzhN-Q8&feature=player_embedded; accessed June 3, 2014. Author's italics.

(miniaturized computers) would be connected to the metabrain; they could repair or even replace any defective body parts. Thus, Primo would be ageless!

The body would be protected by "Smart Skin." This outer covering could be transformed into different appearances and even different materials depending on the environment or a person's mood. Since there would be nanobots throughout the layers of skin, they would be able to communicate sensory data to the metabrain concerning the existing weather conditions. Thus, the colour and the texture of the skin could be adapted to the prevailing temperatures. Toxins in the air and solar radiation could also be monitored and, if needed, removed.

Vita-More designed Primo Posthuman to be highly versatile depending upon a person's activity. She noted:

> For hiking, I would like leg strength, stamina, a skin sheath to protect me from damaging environmental aspects, self-moisturizing, cool-down capability, extended hearing and augmented vision.... For a party, I would like an eclectic look—a glistening bronze skin with emerald green highlights...a sophisticated internal sound system so that I could alter the music to suit my taste."[11]

As scientific discoveries related to nano/bio technologies expand, Dr. Vita-More will be upgrading the capacities of Primo. In designing this posthuman, she has definitely benefitted from being a certified personal trainer and sports nutritionist. To her, a body must be "sustainable and streamlined."[12] She has applied these two principles to her own life by making healthy choices and exercising daily.

---

11 "Natasha Vita-More," *La Spirale* eZine; http://www.laspirale.org/texte.php?id=33; accessed June 3, 2014.

12 "Natasha Vita-More," *La Spirale* eZine.

DEATH—A TRAGEDY

"I have no tolerance for it [death], no time for it. It just makes me angry. It's the cruelest thing to happen to any human being,"[13] voices Natasha Vita-More. Furthermore, she states, "I hold no religious belief. I think religion is not a healthy thing for a society because it has dictums, rules and regulations and I am right; you are wrong."[14] Instead, she has been attracted to Zen Buddhism— not for its beliefs but rather for its zest for life.

The reality of the Grim Reaper's hand struck home on May 31, 1996, when Timothy Leary, a close, personal friend, died. An illustrious psychologist and pioneer in psychedelic therapy, he had been an ardent supporter of cryonics. A year after the founding of the Alcor Life Extension Foundation in 1988, he registered to have his body cryopreserved. Possibly, he had some influence upon Vita-More who did likewise in 1991.

Knowing that death from cancer was imminent in the spring of 1996, he was encouraged to have the equipment set up in his house so that cryopreservation could be started immediately after his demise. But, before his death, as a result of the influence of his family, he changed his mind. Instead, he was cremated and his ashes were distributed among family and friends.

Such a decision was devastating for Natasha. How she wished that Leary had been cryopreserved and that, at least, there would have been the possibility of his escaping the absolute finality of death. Later, she commented:

> My personal feeling is that Tim was very impressionable during the final stages of his life and people who spent a lot of time around him had specific religious beliefs. While cryonicists were trying to be respectful of his privacy, others were trying to influence him.... I suppose Tim

---

13 Brendan Bernhard, "The Transhumanists: Meet Max and Natasha. They Hope to Live Forever. Seriously," *LA Weekly* (January 17, 2001); http://www.laweekly.com/2001-01-25/news/the-transhumanists/; accessed June 3, 2014.

14 Vita-More interviewed by Danaylov on *Singularity 1 on 1* (2011).

is immortal after all, isn't he? *His brilliant and riveting ideas still carry on, if only in digital form.*[15]

With the assistance of modern technology, posthumanists are challenging humanity's greatest enemy—death. No longer should any individual's life be relegated to just memories.

---

15 "Natasha Vita-More," *La Spirale* eZine. Author's italics.

10

THE RESURRECTED BODY
The Christian's hope

NO RESURRECTION IN
THE GRECO-ROMAN WORLD

"**D**eath for those of the first-century Greco-Roman world was a harsh and obvious fact of life that was implacable, and therefore inevitable."[1] Even though it is difficult to be definitive concerning the life span of those living in the first century A.D., New Testament scholar Peter Bolt has estimated that the average life expectancy was "about twenty-two years for men and twenty years for women...that only 40 per cent of the population reached that age [early twenties]; and that only 50 per cent of the children made it to their tenth birthday."[2]

---

1 Peter Bolt, "Life, Death and the Afterlife in the Greco-Roman World," in *Life in the Face of Death: The Resurrection Message of the New Testament*, ed. Richard Longenecker (Grand Rapids: Eerdmans, 1998), 63. "Death was felt as a grievous loss both to the dying and to the bereaved" in N.T. Wright, *The Resurrection of the Son of God* (Fortress Press: Minneapolis, 2003), 82.

2 Bolt, "Life, Death and the Afterlife in the Greco-Roman World," 52.

Gripped not only with the brevity of life, but also with the dread and uncertainties surrounding death, most people of the first century believed in the immortality of the soul. They were greatly influenced by Homer (c. 850 B.C), the greatest epic poet, and also Aeschylus (525 B.C.–456 B.C), an Athenian playwright. Both these men emphatically announced that the resurrection of the body was an impossibility. The latter, in his play, *Eumenides*, had the god Apollo state: "Once a man has died, and the dust has soaked up his blood, there is no resurrection (*anastasis*)."[3]

The Greco-Roman world thoroughly embraced the belief that a person's body was reduced to dust at death and, thus, belief in resurrection was untenable. What prompted this society to adopt such a philosophical position? The human body with its distressing physical limitations and its painful infirmities was viewed as repulsive and a hindrance. In reality, "the body was a mere husk, the prison of the soul, and it is not until death of the body that the soul can begin its real life."[4]

Furthermore, the soul, a non-material and immortal entity, "existed before the body, and will continue to exist after the body is gone."[5] Consequently, it is understandable that those living in the ancient world, viewing the body as they did, would have the deceased immediately cremated after death.

Since the soul was immediately released from the body, it was believed that, by doing so, his or her soul would enter "the Underworld or Hades faster than through burial in the ground."[6] But the soul's journey to the elysium fields, a tropical paradise, was dark and foreboding at best.

---

3 *Eumenides*, 647f, as quoted by Wright, *The Resurrection of the Son of God*, 32.

4 Ernie Bradford, *Paul: The Traveller* (London: Allan Lane, 1974), 104.

5 Wright, *The Resurrection of the Son of God*, 49.

6 David Herbert, *Eternity Before Their Eyes, Worldviews Examined: The Apostle Paul in Athens and Modern University Students* (London: D&I Herbert, 2007), 52.

THE RESURRECTION: A FOUNDATIONAL CHRISTIAN TRUTH

> But if there is no resurrection (*anastasis*) of the dead, not even Christ has been raised; and if Christ has not been raised, then our preaching is vain, your faith also is vain (kenē).[7]

No one living today could ever imagine or appreciate how liberating the resurrection (*anastasis*) message was to the Greco-Roman mind. These people daily witnessed the grim and stark reality of death. To be told that Jesus Christ, the God-man, had conquered death by means of his resurrection brought hope and peace.

The central theme of this "Good News" or *euaggelion*[8] was that, by an act of faith prior to death, they too could one day possess a resurrected body that would be similar to that of the risen Christ,[9] not for a mere twenty years or so, but eternally.

Unlike the view of the prevailing culture, why did the early Christians cherish the human body and not despise it?[10] They believed the scriptural accounts as recorded in Genesis, that God, the author of life, "created man in his own image, in the image of God he created him: male and female he created them."[11]

Furthermore, this act of creation is more fully delineated in the next chapter when it states: "Then God formed man of the dust of the ground and breathed into his nostrils the breath of life and man became a living being."[12] Thus, the human body, so exquisitely and marvelously designed, was a miraculous creation of God.[13] But why then is this body now subject to the three dreaded "Ds of life": disease, death and decay?

---

7 1 Corinthians 15:13–14.

8 *Euaggelion* is composed of *eu* (good) and *aggelos* (a messenger).

9 See Romans 8:29; 2 Corinthians 3:18; Colossians 3:10.

10 "For no one ever hated his own flesh, but nourishes and cherishes it" (Ephesians 5:29).

11 Genesis 1:27.

12 Genesis 2:7.

13 "I will give thanks to You, for I am fearfully and wonderfully made" (Psalm 139:14).

These unfortunate eventualities did not originate from the hand of God, but were a result of the willful disobedience of his first created pair, Adam and Eve. "Man's mortality was not a consequence of his creation but of his sin."[14] In writing to the Christians in Rome, the apostle Paul captured very succinctly the nature of the problem: "Therefore, just as through one man [Adam] sin entered into the world, and death through sin, and so death spread to all men because all sinned."[15]

The entrance of sin into the world, as one would expect, caused an unyielding rift between God, the essence of perfection, and humanity under the domination of sin. In describing the effects that sin had on the body, the apostle Paul states : "The outer man is decaying (*diaphtheipetai*).... For, indeed, in this *house* we groan...."[16] The verbal form of *diaphtheirō* is in the passive mood.[17] In other words, sin was the force that was causing "the outer body" to groan as it experienced the infirmities and the accompanying pain of life.

From a biblical perspective, every human is a tripartite being: body, soul and spirit.[18] Each of these areas has not escaped the ravages of sin, but each is fully functional, especially the spirit which bears the image of God. The spirit has not been lost "but merely tarnished or distorted. It does not need to be regained but to be perfectly restored/renewed."[19]

That God does have a high regard for the body is best illustrated by the fact that God the Son, Jesus Christ, took on a human form. "And the Word (*Logos*) became flesh and dwelt among (*eskēnōsen*)

---

14 Murray J. Harris, *Raised Immortal: Resurrection and Immortality in the New Testament* (Grand Rapids: Eerdmans, 1983), 192.

15 Romans 5:12.

16 2 Corinthians 4:16; 5:2.

17 The same thought is conveyed in 2 Corinthians 5:1: "For we know that if the earthly tent which is our house is torn down (*kataluthē*)." *Kataluthē* is from the verbal form, *kataluō*, and is also in the passive mood.

18 1 Thessalonians 5:23. Some Christians believe that human beings are composed of two distinct components, material and immaterial: body and soul.

19 Roy E. Ciampa and Brian S. Rosner, *The First Letter to the Corinthians* (Grand Rapids: Eerdmans, 2010), 824.

us and we beheld his glory."[20] Jesus, the *Logos*, was God's Word or communication between himself and humankind.

Furthermore, the apostle John deliberately chose the verb *skēnoō* to describe Jesus' life among the people of Palestine. The root of *skēnoō* is *skēnē*, meaning tent or, more specifically, the Tent or the Tabernacle of the Old Testament. As the children of Israel lived in the desert for forty years, they witnessed the presence of God as he met with them in the Tabernacle, located in the centre of their camp.

Jesus, the same God that led the children of Israel in the wilderness, now "tabernacled" or lived with the Jewish people of the first century A.D. Shamefully, these Jews, blinded by their own sin, failed to acknowledge him as the incarnate God who came to address their greatest need—to be saved from their sins.

THE NATURE OF THE RESURRECTED BODY
The apostle Paul, the most prolific writer of the New Testament, provided the most comprehensive information concerning the resurrection of the body. In his second letter to the church in Corinth, he wrote:

> For we know that if the earthly tent (*skēnos*) which is our house is torn down, we have a building (*oikodomē*) from God, a house not made with hands, eternal in the heavens.[21]

As illustrated in Table 1, the "earthly tent" (*skēnos*)[22] or physical body, marred by the effects of sin, is characterized as being perishable, inglorious and weak.[23] At death, this earthly frame is destined to destruction. In its place, each believer will be given a resurrected body by God himself. In constrast, this new body will be imperishable, glorious and powerful.

---

20 John 1:14.
21 2 Corinthians 5:1.
22 It is the same term used for Jesus' body as seen in John 1:14.
23 1 Corinthians 15:42-44.

To demonstrate the eternal nature of this new spiritual (*pneumatikos*) body, Paul refers to this new creation as a building as opposed to a tent. "The resurrected believer will have a heavenly body that is incapable of deterioration, beautiful in form and appearance, and with limitless energy and perfect health."[24]

Table 1 also shows that the soul and spirit[25] of a person who has come to faith in Jesus Christ is totally unaffected by death. This spiritual continuity is comprised of a believer's personal qualities (soul) and spiritual identity (spirit) in Christ. In the presence of the Lord, one will be recognized and welcomed by family and friends. This joyous reunion will last for an eternity.

Randy Alcorn, in his excellent book, *Heaven*, explores this theme of a spiritual continuum between this life and the life to come. He maintains that soul and spirit possessed by every believer is the defining essence of life. Commenting upon how one's resurrected body and soul and spirit could operate in total harmony, this popular author and conference speaker has made an insightful observation:

> What makes *you*? It's not only your body but also your memory, personality, traits, gifts, passions, preferences, and interests. In the final resurrection, I believe all of these facets will be restored and amplified, untarnished by sin and the Curse.[26]

As a source of encouragement, the apostle Paul made reference to the fact that God has given each believer in Christ "the Spirit as a pledge (*arrhabōn*)."[27] This Greek word was a commercial term that denoted the down payment for something purchased. Such a deposit or partial payment signified that the transaction was considered to be completed by both parties involved and that further

---

24 Harris, *Raised Immortal*, 121.

25 The soul can be defined as one's intelligence, creativity, will and emotions while the spirit is one's capacity to worship—whether it be God, one's self or material things.

26 Randy Alcorn, *Heaven* (Wheaton: Tyndale, 2004), 274. Italics in the original.

27 2 Corinthians 5:5.

PHYSICAL STATE	Death	RESURRECTED STATE

Soul and spirit (personal qualities / spiritual identity) ——————————————————————————→

Earthly body ------- Destruction -----→ Resurrected body ——————→
1. Perishable   1. Imperishable
2. Inglorious   2. Glorious
3. Weak   3. Powerful

Death

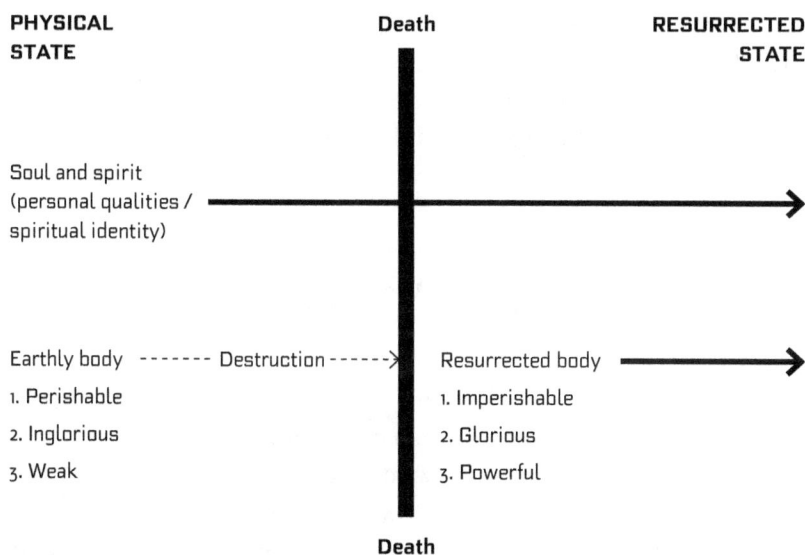

Table 1. From a physical state to a resurrected state for all believers.

payments were forthcoming. Similarly, in modern Greek, "the engagement ring is *arrhabōna*"—the first step of commitment toward a future marriage.[28]

Likewise, the Spirit, God's pledge or *arrhabōn*, is the agent of continuity between this age and the age to come. In this age, not only does he confirm that a believer is a child of God, but through his Word, he is daily transforming each one into the image of the risen Christ. But when the time comes to be ushered into the age to come, it will be the Spirit who miraculously clothes each believer with his or her resurrection body.

JESUS' RESURRECTED BODY

Since death was introduced as a result of Adam's act of blatant disobedience, this enemy of life has been relentless and formidable

---

28 Harris, *Raised Immortal*, 142.

in that it has had total mastery over every human being. Then, Jesus Christ, the God-man, burst forth into human history. At his crucifixion on Mount Calvary, he willingly submitted himself into death's clutches; but, three days later, he emerged triumphantly, to which the apostle Paul quoted the prophets Isaiah and Hosea in this paean of praise:

"Death is swallowed up in victory."
"O death, where is your victory?
O death, where is your sting?"[29]

Jesus' risen body had undergone some radical changes. "He was no longer bound by material or spatial limitations."[30] He suddenly appeared before his disciples who had barricaded themselves in a closed room for fear of the Jewish authorities.[31] But he bore the wound marks and scars. "The point was that there was continuity between Jesus' old body and the new one. It was the old body that had been raised and transformed by God's resurrection power."[32]

In his incredible treatise on the resurrection, sent to the church in Corinth, Paul mentioned that there were three specific appearances by Jesus: first, to his disciples; second, to an assembly of 500; and, finally, to Paul himself. But it is the gospel writers who have left the most intimate details of Jesus' interaction with his disciples following his resurrection.

In Luke's Gospel, Jesus encountered two of his disciples on the road to Emmaus which was about 11 km (7 mi) from Jerusalem. Fearful of the coming reprisals by the Jewish leaders, and distraught that Jesus, the long-awaited Messiah, was dead, they were fleeing for their lives. During their time together, as they were walking along, the two never realized that it was Jesus. But he

---

29 1 Corinthians 15:54–55. See Isaiah 25:8 and Hosea 13:14.

30 Harris, *Raised Immortal*, 53.

31 John 20:19.

32 Ben Witherington III, *Revelation and the End Times: Unraveling God's Message of Hope* (Nashville: Abingdon, 2010), 112.

gave them one of the most amazing Bible lessons. "Beginning with Moses and with all the prophets, he explained to them the things concerning himself in all the Scriptures."[33] Such inspirational teaching resonated well within them.

But the turning point of this unforgettable experience occurred when, during the evening meal in their home, their eyes were opened and they immediately recognized him as Jesus, after which he disappeared. No longer despondent, but rather filled with excitement, they went back to Jerusalem to inform the other disciples that the Lord had really risen.[34]

In his masterful letter to the church in Rome, Paul forcefully set in juxtaposition two of Jesus' greatest feats: his incarnation (becoming man) and his resurrection:

> Concerning his Son who was born of a descendant of David according to the flesh, who was *declared the Son of God* with power by the resurrection from the dead, according to the Spirit of holiness, Jesus Christ our Lord.[35]

Jesus' title, "Lord," separates him from all other religious leaders. Unlike our modern transhumanists who view death as a disease to be cured, Jesus knew it to be an enemy.[36] Since his earthly father, Joseph, was never mentioned after his twelfth birthday, it would appear that he witnessed Joseph's death.

But life, even a long and productive one, is a gift from God. "Yet it is not surviving—living a long life *per se*—that makes this blessing a good gift. It is rather the extended opportunity to worship and serve Christ, to love God and neighbour that makes the gift good."[37]

---

33 Luke 24:27.

34 Luke 24:33.

35 Romans 1:3–4. Author's italics.

36 "The last enemy that will be abolished is death" (1 Corinthians 15:26).

37 Brent Waters, *This Mortal Flesh: Incarnation and Bioethics* (Grand Rapids: Brazos, 2009), 147.

THE TRANSHUMANISTS' HOPE:
A DIGITAL HEAVEN

Some two thousand years later, the transhumanists' disdain toward their bodies is strikingly similar to that of those living in the first century A.D. The modern explanation for the frailties of the body is attributed to natural selection. During the evolutionary process, the human body was designed to atrophy or wear out. To rectify this universal deterioration, transhumanists are eagerly awaiting the Singularity, dated to be around 2050, at which time the merging of the body with advanced technologies will occur.

Denis Alexander, Director of the Faraday Institute for Science and Religion at Cambridge University, has summarized the transhumanists' aspirations as follows:

> The messianic hope in this case is placed in technology that will shape the enhanced, better human, perhaps a new species altogether, the posthuman. And then in the far future lies the hope of immortality when the posthuman will become substrate-independent, delivered from the constraints of flesh and blood *to live on in a digital heaven.*[38]

---

38 Denis Alexander, "Enhancing Humans or a New Creation?" *The Jubilee Centre* (June 2009); http://www.jubilee-centre.org/enhancing-humans-or-a-new-creation/; accessed June 4, 2014. Author's italics.

11

CONCLUSION

A March 2013 article in *Digital Trends*, "How One Russian Millionaire Wants to Save the World...With Immortal Cyborgs," announced that the second annual Global Future 2045 Congress would be held in New York during the third weekend of June. Dmitry Itskov, a thirty-two-year-old Russian mogul, "who made his fortune as founder of the Web publishing company New Media Stars," would be its organizer.[1] He had previously conducted his first Congress in Moscow the year before.

The promotional video for the June conference, titled, "2045: A New Era for Humanity," made these bold pronouncements:

Yet what we need is not just a new technological revolution but a new civilization or paradigm; we need a new

---

1 Andrew Couts, "How One Russian Millionaire Wants to Save the World...With Immortal Cyborgs," *Digital Trends* (March 26, 2013); http://www.digitaltrends.com/cool-tech/dmitry-itskov-2045-initiative/#!T4508; accessed June 3, 2014.

philosophy and ideology, new ethics, new culture, new psychology and even a new metaphysics. We must reset our limits and go beyond ourselves, beyond the earth and beyond the solar system. This is an adequate response to the challenges of our time. Thus, a new reality and future man will arise.[2]

Desiring to explore and understand the implications of "this new reality," Dmitry Itskov invited thirty-three leading transhumanists whose expertise focused on the fields of "technology, business, research and spirituality"[3] to be presenters at the conference.[4] Included among those who spoke were Ray Kurzweil and Natasha Vita-More. New York's prestigious Lincoln Center provided ample room and comfort for the 800 attendees who paid a registration fee of $750 each.[5]

The conference's motto was "On the Path to a New Evolutionary Strategy," which was highlighted by Itskov's four-staged Avatar Project. This Russian visionary believed that the overall aim of Global Future 2045 was to create an awareness of the coming technologies that will enable "the transfer of an individual's personality to a more advanced non-biological carrier and [will] extend life to the point of immortality."[6]

Canadian transhumanist Nikola Danaylov attended the conference, where he met one of the speakers, Nigel Ackland. After hearing his presentation, Danaylov decided that he had to interview

---

2   "2045: A New Era for Humanity" (May 2013); http://youtu.be/CDnSP1eCR68; accessed June 2, 2014. This video was used to advertise Russia 2045, the first Global Future 2045 congress, held in Moscow in 2012.

3   Daniel Faggella, "A Review of the 2nd Global Future 2045 Conference in New York City," Institute for Emerging Ethics and Technologies (June 28, 2013); http://ieet.org/index.php/IEET/more/faggella20130628; accessed June 2, 2014.

4   For a complete list of speakers and their biographical information, see http://gf2045.com/speakers/; accessed June 2, 2014.

5   Faggella, "A Review of the 2nd Global Future 2045 Conference."

6   "What is the 2045 Initiative All About?" *33rd Square* (April 23, 2013); http://www.33rdsquare.com/2013/04/what-is-2045-initiative-all-about.html; accessed June 3, 2014.

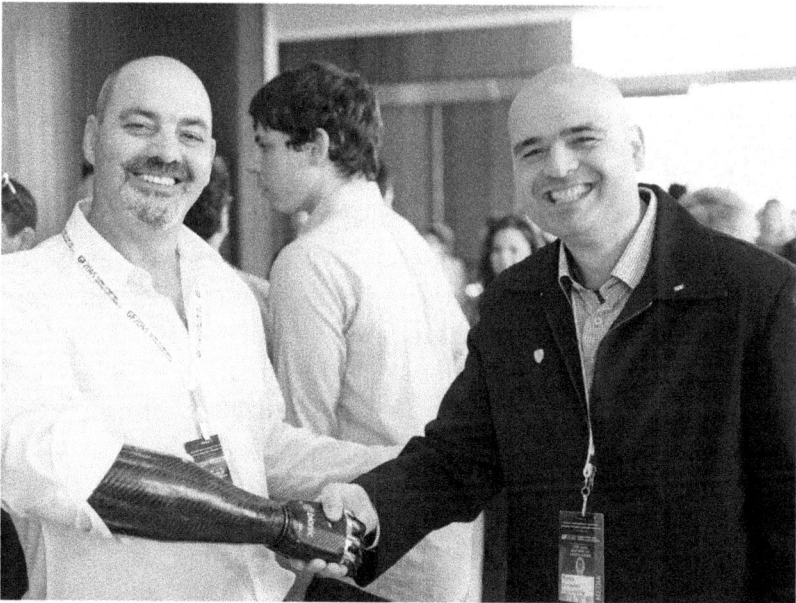

Nigel Ackland with Nikola Danaylow at the 2045 Congress in New York City.
© Nikola Danaylov. Used with permission.

him for his program, *Singularity 1 on 1*. Early in the interview, Danaylov made this comment: "In my opinion, he [Nigel] had the most moving of all the presentations, and it was titled, "Ordinary... Extraordinary: Life with a Bionic Arm.""[7]

In 2006, Ackland, a British subject, was involved in a traumatic accident. As a smelter of precious metal was being moved, he had his right arm caught and severed in an industrial blending machine. After six years of trying various arm prosthetics, he was directed to the RSLSteeper company; here, he was outfitted with a bionic arm. He stated:

> Having a bebionic hand is like being human again; psychologically I would not be without it. I can hold the phone,

7   Nigel Ackland interviewed by Nikola Danaylov on *Singularity 1 on 1*; "Ordinary... Extraordinary: Life with a Bionic Arm" (June 2013); http://www.singularityweblog.com/ nigel-ackland-bionic-arm/; accessed June 3, 2014.

shake hands and wash my left hand normally, which I have
not been able to do for five years. I am back to being a
two-finger typist.... Overall, the bebionic hand has had a
great impact on my life; not only does it look more like a
human hand but it also functions more like a human hand.[8]

Why was Nigel Ackland, a man with an amazing prosthetic arm,
at a conference focusing on self-directed evolutionary progress
which would eventually lead to human immortality? The media
attention, which Nigel's bebionic arm inevitably drew, reinforced
the humanitarian image that transhumanism had already established through the efforts of Ray Kurzweil and Kevin Warwick, to
mention two. It is expected that such favourable publicity will
bode well in the years to come. Such conditioning will assist the
general public to accept the transhumanist agenda as it begins to
unfold.

Typically, transhumanists have a definite penchant for distanc-
ing themselves from anything remotely connected to religious
activity. But Robert Geraci, professor of Religious Studies at
Manhattan College, New York, in his excellent article concerning
the interfacing of brains and machines noted: "Transhumanism is
a variation on religious naturalism, an attempt to acquire the traditional goals of religion without recourse to supernatural entities."[9]

Giulio Prisco (b. 1957), physicist and former senior manager of
the European Space Administration, is extremely sympathetic to
the inclusion of spirituality within the transhumanist agenda
advocated by Dmitry Itskov. In a 2011 interview, he clearly sub-
stantiated his position:

---

8   "Patient Stories," RSLSteeper website; http://bebionic.com/the_hand/patient_stor-
ies/nigel_ackland; accessed June 3, 2014.

9   Robert M. Geraci, "Cyborgs, Robots and Eternal Avatars: Transhumanist Salvation
at the Interface of Brains and Machines" in *The Routledge Companion to Religion and
Science*, ed. James W. Haag, Gregory R. Peterson and Michael L. Spezio (London: Routledge, 2012), 585.

Our universe is a very big place with lots of undiscovered and unimagined "things in heaven and earth" which science will uncover someday, and perhaps in this mysterious and beautiful complexity there is room for spirituality and even for the old promises of religions, such as immortality and resurrection.[10]

In 2008, he was one of the founding members of the Order of Cosmic Engineers (OCE).[11] Four years later, Dr. Prisco penned the "Prospectus of the OCE." This techno-salvation document articulated that the OCE "offers no articles of faith, no beliefs, no points of dogma."[12] Being a conviction-based organization, it wants to be recognized as being "UNreligious." During an interview on *Singularity 1 on 1*, Prisco explained this newly coined word:

By UNreligion, we mean something that has the good parts of religion without having the bad parts...to design a complete worldview is something very ambitious. To replace religion in the hearts and minds of people and to give them happiness...based on our scientific understanding of the world while at the same time able to give the same benefits that religions give—hope—hope in immortality and future resurrection and a sense of meaning and a sense of wonder at the marvelous universe we live in.[13]

---

10 Ben Goertzel, "Technological Transcendence: An Interview with Giulio Prisco," *H+ Magazine* (February 8, 2011); http://hplusmagazine.com/2011/02/08/technological-transcendence-an-interview-with-giulio-prisco/; accessed June 3, 2014.

11 See "Order of Cosmic Engineers" for a complete list: http://wikibin.org/index2.php?option=com_content&do_pdf=1&id=21409; accessed June 3, 2014. One is not surprised to find the names of such transhumanists as William Sims Bainbridge, Ben Goertzel, Max More, Natasha Vita-More and Howard Bloom.

12 Giulio Prisco, "Order of Cosmic Engineers," *Turing Church Magazine* (January 12, 2012); http://turingchurch.com/2012/01/02/order-of-cosmic-engineers/; accessed June 3, 2014.

13 Giulio Prisco interviewed by Nikola Danaylov on *Singularity 1 on 1*; "The End Is Not the End" (2013); http://www.singularityweblog.com/giulio-prisco-on-singularity-1-on-1/; accessed June 3, 2014.

Furthermore, from a biblical perspective, the desire for transhumanists to become as/like God is not new. Was it not Satan
who said to our first parents: "For God knows that in the day you
eat from it, your eyes will be opened, and you will be like God,
knowing good and evil"?[14]

The apostle John, in the final book of the Bible, Revelation,
outlined the events that will occur in the final stages of world
history. In Revelation 12, John introduced the evil triumverate:
Satan, the anti-Christ and the false prophet. John's focus was directed toward the first two when he wrote:

> And the dragon [Satan] gave him [anti-Christ] his power
> and his throne and great authority. I *saw* one of his heads
> as if it had been slain, and his fatal wound was healed.
> And the whole earth was amazed *and followed* after the
> beast; they worshipped the dragon because he gave his
> authority to the beast; and they worshipped the beast.
> saying, "Who is able to wage war with him?"[15]

Is this passage—which captures themes such as death, immortality
and world domination—referring to the role that transhumanism
would play in the latter days of the earth's history? If transhumanism, with its amazing achievements, continues to captivate the
attention of people worldwide, is there a possibility that this anti-
Christian religion could become Satan's last weapon to challenge
God, and subsequently be utterly defeated?

Such a defeat will happen when the "Christian Singularity"
occurs. All avenues of history have been converging toward it—
the return of the Lord Jesus Christ. At that time, Jesus will bring
his righteous judgement to bear upon all evil actions of humanity.
To his followers, Jesus gave this forewarning concerning pseudo-
saviours and futurists: "For false Christs and false prophets will

---

14 Genesis 3:5.
15 Revelation 13:2–4.

arise and will show signs and wonders, so as to mislead, if possible, even the elect."[16]

But it is the last two chapters of the book of Revelation that provide the greatest sense of hope to those who have been reconciled to God through Jesus' death and resurrection for their sins.[17] To that end, John wrote:

> ...he [God] will dwell among them, and they shall be his people, and God himself will be among them, and he will wipe away every tear from their eyes; *and there will be no longer any death*; there will no longer be any mourning, or crying, or pain; the first things have passed away.[18]

In summary, Dónal O'Mathúna, a senior lecturer in ethics at Dublin University, has made this insightful observation about the quest to transcend beyond humanity:

> The biblical account claims God had a goal in mind, making humans according to his own image.... Posthumanists would have us believe that they can start with the raw material of existing human beings and fashion them into posthumans, *made in the image of themselves*."[19]

---

16 Matthew 24:24.

17 2 Corinthians 5:21.

18 Revelation 21:3–4. Author's italics.

19 Dónal P. O'Mathúna, *Nanoethics: Big Ethical Issues with Small Technology* (London: Continuum, 2009),176. Author's italics.

APPENDIX
Transhumanist questionnaire

O n a sunny day, August 7, 2011, four people ventured into Victoria Park in London, Ontario, to begin the transhumanist questionnaire.[1] For the first time in six-and-a-half years, a questionnaire was not being conducted only on the sidewalks outside the University of Western Ontario (UWO) but rather across the city.

Nine months later at UWO, my son, Trent, and I were asking individuals if they would answer three questions related to the transhumanist questionnaire. Trent approached a student from China studying English as a second language,[2] and I approached a Canadian graduate student in music.[3] They both agreed to participate.

What is significant about these two students is that they both stated that they were not religious. Their response was very

---

1 The questionnaire was completed on May 29, 2014.
2 Interview #546 (April 4, 2013).
3 Interview #547 (April 4, 2013).

common and typical. By further prompting from the author, the Canadian graduate music student expanded his reasons for considering himself non-religious. Being an atheist, he indicated that he had absolutely no interest in church, reading the Bible or praying. In his mind, these factors definitely defined a religious person. Since they were not part of his life, he naturally considered himself to be non-religious.

In the past five questionnaires we have conducted for various projects, the answer "none" or "not stated" has always rated high when asked if a person had a religious persuasion.[4] But in the present transhumanist questionnaire, 19.25% of respondents classified themselves as having no religious connections (see Table 2). To further substantiate this lack of religious affiliation, I chose to compare two surveys: one Canadian and the other American.

According to Statistics Canada's 2011 National Household Survey, "Roughly 7,850,600 people, or nearly one-quarter of Canada's population (23.9%), had no religious affiliation. This was up from 16.5% a decade earlier, as recorded in the 2001 census."[5] Even more revealing is that in 1991, the percentage was 12%.[6]

In the United States, the Cooperative Institutional Research Program (CIRP) began to survey first-year college students concerning their societal opinions and attitudes in 1968. The first year of the survey found that 10% of the students stated that they had no religious affiliation. In 1978, it dropped to its lowest point of 8.3%

Allen Downey, associate professor of computer science at the Franklin W. Olin College of Engineering, has been tracking freshmen's responses concerning their religious preference for a number of years. He discovered that in 2011 the percentage rose to

4   See, for example, David Herbert, *Eternity Before Their Eyes, Worldviews Examined: The Apostle Paul in Athens and Modern University Students* (London: D & I Herbert, 2007).

5   Statistics Canada, "2011 National Household Survey: Immigration, Place of Birth, Citizenship, Ethnic Origin, Visible Minorities, Language and Religion"; http://www.statcan.gc.ca/daily-quotidien/130508/dq130508b-eng.htm; accessed June 4, 2014.

6   Michael Valpy and Joe Friesen, "Canada Marching from Religion to Secularization," *The Globe and Mail* (August 23, 2012); http://www.theglobeandmail.com/news/national/canada-marching-from-religion-to-secularization/article1320108/; accessed June 4, 2014.

Table 2. Religious persuasion

None / Not stated	154	Supreme Being	17
Roman Catholic	133	Greek Orthodox	12
Protestant	105	Sikh	4
Atheist	103	Jewish	4
Agnostic	74	Native American	4
Muslim	47	Pantheist	2
Evangelical	44	Confuscianist	1
Theist	43	Satanist	1
Spiritual	19	Taoist	1
Buddhist	15	Other	3
Hindu	14		
		Total	800

24%. Based on the past statistics, he was confident that, in the following years, the percentage would continue to increase.

In 2012, CIRP surveyed 190,000 students from 283 colleges. In an article, "Freshman hordes regress to the mean,"[7] Dr. Downey was totally surprised when he learned that the 2012 results actually took a slight unexpected dip to 23.8%.

What might account for this considerable growth from 8% in 1978 to 23.8% in 2012? Dr. Downey earlier suggested one possible contributing factor: "This jump may be due to increased visibility of atheism following the publication of books by Sam Harris [b. 1967], Daniel Dennett [b. 1942] and Richard Dawkins."[8]

Books by these "new atheists" are definitely having an impact: *The End of Faith* (2004) by Sam Harris, *Darwin's Dangerous Idea*

7 Allen Downey, "Freshman Hordes Regress to the Mean" (April 9, 2013); http://allendowney.blogspot.ca/2013/04/freshman-hordes-regress-to-mean.html; accessed June 4, 2014.

8 Allen Downey, "The Godless Freshman," *The Council for Secular Humanism* (July 17, 2007); http://www.secularhumanism.org/index.php?section=library&page=downey_27_5; accessed June 4, 2014.

(1996) by Daniel Dennett and, most notable, *The God Delusion* (2006) by Richard Dawkins. Dawkins' book was on the bestseller list for almost a year and has sold some two million copies.[9]

QUESTION #1

What would you do if the opportunity of receiving a brain-chip implant was offered to you in order to improve your mental and physical capabilities? It is expected that this enhancement could substantially improve your academic performance (or the possibility for advancement in your place of employment). This procedure would necessitate a reconfiguration of your brain.

A University of Western Ontario graduate student, wanting to pursue a doctorate both in science and medicine, was in favour of receiving the brain-chip. He said that the mere thought of having the implant was "incredibly enticing." This brilliant student felt that, by having this device, it would enhance his ability to conduct research.[10] A construction coordinator believed that, if a person had the implant, this individual would have a definite advantage over one's peers which was needed in these competitive times.[11]

On the other hand, walking into Victoria Park, I was greeted by a busker touting a banjo.[12] This young man with demonic tattoos on his arm was adamantly opposed to having the chip placed within his head. Futhermore, he would not use any medicine and would refuse a blood transfusion even if it meant his death. Interestingly, his interpretation of the temptation story in Genesis 3 was totally consistent with his satanic worldview. Satan was viewed as the liberator who granted Adam and Eve freedom of choice while God, the villain, wanted to force his will on our first parents and, thus, to restrict their personal choice.

---

9 Stephen Bullivant, "The New Atheism and Sociology," in Amarnath Amarasingam, ed., *Religion and the New Atheism: A Critical Appraisal* (Leiden: Brill, 2010), 116.

10 Interview #225 (February 23, 2013).

11 Interview #126 (October 30, 2011).

12 Interview #569 (May 15, 2013).

Table 3. Results regarding brain-chip implant (question 1).

I would agree to accept the brain-chip implant	146
I would not accept the brain-chip implant	466
I am undecided as to what to do	188
Total	800

The overwhelming majority, as seen in Table 3, was very skeptical of the benefits that could be accrued through an implant. It was commonly deemed unnatural and dangerous. One student who was majoring in computer studies indicated: "Individuals will become too dependent on technology and will lose their personal initiative."[13]

The possibility of losing personal autonomy and the question of control was voiced frequently. An artist raised another extremely valid concern: What would happen if the implant was attacked by computer viruses?[14]

QUESTION #2

Do you believe that the transhumanist goal of ultimately eliminating death is possible?

As a segue from the first question to this one (see Table 4), I would mention that transhumanists believe that, by merging technology and humanity, immortality can be attained. Those who believe that transhumanists would eliminate death agreed with a second-year history student that, with the advancements in technology, it was just a matter of time before death would be conquered.[15]

A retired university president doubted that the transhumanist goal could be achieved. He personally believed that, since people

---

13 Interview #533 (March 1, 2013).

14 Interview #185 (December 22, 2011).

15 Interview #67 (September 22, 2011).

are spiritual beings, there must be some type of afterlife.[16] A philosophy student clearly articulated the view of the majority: "I think it is possible, but the question is whether it is desirable. The inevitability of death spurs people into action."[17]

QUESTION #3
What, do you think, will happen to people when they die?

Between 2005 and 2007, for my book, *Eternity Before Their Eyes*, 1,200 students were questioned about their beliefs concerning what would happen when they die; the results at that time were as follows:

Heaven or Hell (47.5%)   Reincarnation (8.4%)
Cessation of existence (21.3%)   Spiritual continuum (4.3%)
Do not know (15.1%)   Other (3.5%)[18]

Seven years later, there have been significant changes in the three largest categories as noted in Table 5. Here are some percentages from our present study, for comparison:

Heaven or Hell [top three combined] (33.6%)
Cessation of Existence (23%)
Do not know (25.1%)

One important fact can be adduced from this comparison: there has been a dramatic increase in the uncertainty of, or even skepticism of, what happens to individuals after death. There can be no doubt that a key contributing factor could be that our Western society, formerly committed to a supernatural worldview, has become more committed to a naturalistic or humanistic one.

---

16 Interview #29 (September 11, 2011).
17 Interview #54 (September 22, 2011).
18 Herbert, *Eternity Before Their Eyes*, 98.

Table 4. Results regarding the elimination of death (question 2).

Strongly agree	45
Agree	194
No opinion	67
Disagree	298
Strongly disagree	196
Total	800

Table 5. Results regarding death (question 3).

Heaven or Hell	198
Purgatory	43
Heaven (Hell and Purgatory do not exist)	28
Reincarnation	81
Cessation of existence	184
Do not know	201
Other	65
Total	800

SELECT BIBLIOGRAPHY

ARTICLES

Bostrom, Nick. "A History of Transhumanist Thought," *Journal of Evolution and Technology* 14 (2009): 1–25.

Lee, Earl. "Francis Schaeffer: Prophet of the Religious Right," *The Humanist* 48 (September/October 1988): 28–29.

Pfeffer, Leo. "How Religious Is Secular Humanism?" *The Humanist* 48 (September/October 1988): 13–18, 50.

Wilson, Edwin H. "The Origins of Modern Humanism," *The Humanist* 51 (January/February 1991): 9–11, 28.

BOOKS

Allhoff, Fritz, Patrick Lin and Daniel Moore. *What Is Nanotechnology and Why Does It Matter? From Science to Ethics.* West Sussex: Wiley-Blackwell, 2010.

Bainbridge, William Sims. *Nanoconvergence: The Unity of Nanoscience, Biotechnology, Information Technology, and Cognitive Science.* Upper Saddle River: Prentice Hall, 2007.

Barnett, Paul William. *The Second Epistle to the Corinthians*. Grand Rapids: Eerdmans, 1997.

Brown, Callum G., ed. *The Death of Christian Britain: Understanding Secularisation*. London: Routledge, 2002.

Buchanan, Allen E. *Beyond Humanity? The Ethics of Biomedical Enhancement*. Oxford: Oxford University Press, 2011.

Cave, Stephen. *Immortality: The Quest to Live Forever and How It Drives Civilization*. New York: Crown, 2012.

Ciampa, Roy E. and Brian S. Rosner. *The First Letter to the Corinthians*. Grand Rapids: Eerdmans, 2010.

Cooke, Bill. *A Wealth of Insights: Humanist Thought Since the Enlightenment*. Amherst: Prometheus, 2011.

Cooney, Brian. *Posthumanity: Thinking Philosophically About the Future*. Lanham: Rowman & Littlefield, 2004.

Copeland, B. Jack and others, ed. *Colossus: The Secrets of Bletchley Park's Codebreaking Computers*. Oxford: Oxford University Press, 2006.

de la Mettrie, Julien Offray. *Machine Man and Other Writings*. Trans. and ed. Ann Thomson. Cambridge: Cambridge University Press, 1996.

Dewey, John. *A Common Faith*. New Haven: Yale University Press, 1943.

Dow, Peter B. *Schoolhouse Politics: Lessons from the Sputnik Era*. Cambridge: Harvard University Press, 1991.

Downey, Deane E.D. and Stanley E. Porter, eds. *Christian Worldview and The Academic Disciplines: Crossing the Academy*. Eugene: Pickwick, 2009.

Drexler, K. Eric. *Engines of Creation: The Coming Era of Nanotechnology*. New York: Anchor Press, 1986.

Edmondson III, Henry T. *John Dewey and the Decline of American Education: How the Patron Saint of Schools Has Corrupted Teaching and Learning*. Wilmington: ISI Books, 2006.

Edwards, Jonathan. *A History of the Work of Redemption*. Trans. and ed. John F. Wilson. Vol. 9 of *The Works of Jonathan Edwards*. New Haven: Yale University Press, 1989.

Ettinger, Robert C.W. *The Prospect of Immortality*. New York: Doubleday, 1964.

Flexner, Abraham. *Daniel Coit Gilman: Creator of the American Type of University*. New York: Harcourt, Brace and Co., 1946.

FM-2030. *Are You a Transhuman? Monitoring and Stimulating Your Personal Rate of Growth In a Rapidly Changing World*. New York: Warner, 1989.

Geraci, Robert M. "Cyborgs, Robots and Eternal Avatars: Transhumanist Salvation at the Interface of Brains and Machines" in *The Routledge Companion to Religion and Science*. ed. James W. Haag, Gregory R. Peterson and Michael L. Spezio. London: Routledge, 2011.

Goertzel, Ben and Stephan Vladimir Bugaj. *The Path to Posthumanity: 21st Century Technology and Its Radical Implications for Mind, Society and Reality*. Bethesda: Academica, 2006.

Hall, J. Storrs. *Nanofuture: What's Next for Nanotechnology?* Amherst: Prometheus, 2005.

Hanley, Ryan Patrick and Darrin M. McMahon, eds. *The Enlightenment: Cultural Concepts in Historical Studies*. 5 vols. London: Routledge, 2010.

Harris, John. *Enhancing Evolution: The Ethical Case for Making Better People*. Princeton: Princeton University Press, 2010.

Haycock, David Boyd. *Mortal Coil: A Short History of Living Longer*. New Haven: Yale University Press, 2008.

Heiligman, Deborah. *Charles and Emma: The Darwins' Leap of Faith*. New York: Holt, 2009.

Herbert, David. *Charles Darwin's Religious Views: From Creationist to Evolutionist*. Rev. ed. Kitchener: Joshua Press, 2009.

Herbert, David. *Eternity Before Their Eyes, Worldviews Examined: The Apostle Paul in Athens and Modern University Students*. London: D & I Herbert, 2007.

Herbert, David. *The Faces of Origins: A Historical Survey of the Underlying Assumptions from the Early Church to the Twenty-First Century*. Rev. ed. Kitchener: Joshua Press, 2012.

Herbst, Jurgen. *The German Historical School in American Scholarship: A Study in the Transfer of Culture*. Ithaca: Cornell University Press, 1965.

Kramnick, Isaac, ed. *The Portable Enlightenment Reader*. New York: Penguin, 1995.

Kurtz, Paul. *Embracing the Power of Humanism*. Lanham: Rowman & Littlefield, 2000.

Kurtz, Paul. *Multi-Secularism: A New Agenda*. New Brunswick: Transaction, 2010.

Kurtz, Paul. *Neo-Humanist Statement of Secular Principles and Values: Personal, Progressive and Planetary*. Amherst: Prometheus, 2011.

Kurzweil, Ray. *How to Create a Mind: The Secret of Human Thought Revealed*. New York: Viking, 2012.

Kurzweil, Ray. *The Age of Spiritual Machines*. New York: Viking, 1999.

Kurzweil, Ray. *The Singularity Is Near: When Humans Transcend Biology*. New York: Penguin, 2005.

Laats, Adam. *Fundamentalism and Education in the Scopes Era: God, Darwin, and the Roots of America's Culture Wars*. New York: Palgrave MacMillan, 2010.

Lincoln, Andrew T. *Paradise Now and Not Yet: Studies in the Role of the Heavenly Dimension in Paul's Thought with Special Reference to His Eschatology*. Cambridge: Cambridge University Press, 1981.

Martin, Jay. *The Education of John Dewey: A Biography*. New York: Columbia University Press, 2002.

McManners, John. *Death and the Enlightenment: Changing Attitudes to Death Among Christians and Unbelievers in Eighteenth-Century France*. Oxford: Clarendon, 1981.

More, Max and Natasha Vita-More, eds. *The Transhumanist Reader: Classical and Contemporary Essays on Science, Technology and Philosophy of the Human Future*. Chichester: Wiley-Blackwell, 2013.

Noebel, David A., J.F. Baldwin and Kevin Bywater. *Clergy in the Classroom: The Religion of Secular Humanism*. Rev. 2nd ed. Manitou Springs: Summit Press, 2001.

O'Mathuna, Donal P. *Nanoethics: Big Ethical Issues with Small Technology*. London: Continuum, 2009.

Ryan, Alan. *John Dewey and the High Tide of American Liberalism*. New York: Norton, 1995.

Schwartz, Eilon. *At Home in the World: Human Nature, Ecological Thought and Education after Darwin*. Albany: State University of New York, 2009.

Sellars, Roy Wood. *Religion Coming of Age*. New York: Macmillan, 1928.

Sellars, Roy Wood. *The Next Step in Religion: An Essay Toward the Coming Renaissance*. New York: Macmillan, 1918.

Shea, Victor and William Whitla, eds. *Essays and Reviews: The 1860 Text and Its Reading*. Charlotteville: University of Virginia Press, 2000.

Shook, John R. and Paul Kurtz, eds. *Dewey's Enduring Impact*. Amherst: Prometheus, 2009.

Singham, Mano. *God vs. Darwin: The War Between Evolution and Creationism in the Classroom*. Lanham: Rowman & Littlefield, 2009.

Smith, Graeme. *A Short History of Secularism*. London: I.B. Tauris, 2008.

Warwick, Kevin. *Artificial Intelligence: The Basics*. London: Routledge, 2012.

Warwick, Kevin. *March of the Machines*. London: Century, 1997.

Waters, Brent. *From Human to Posthuman: Christian Theology and Technology in a Postmodern World*. Farnham: Ashgate, 2006.

Waters, Brent. *This Mortal Flesh: Incarnation and Bioethics*. Grand Rapids: Brazo, 2009.

Weiner, Jonathan. *Long for This World: The Strange Science of Immortality*. New York: HarperCollins, 2011.

Wellman, Kathleen. *La Mettrie: Medicine, Philosophy and Enlightenment*. Durham: Duke University Press, 1932.

Wilson, Edwin H. *The Genesis of a Human Manifesto*. Amherst: Humanist Press, 1995.

VIDEOS, FILMS AND DOCUMENTARIES

"Be Who You Would Like To Be." Ray Kurzweil interviewed by Nikola Danaylov on *Singularity 1 on 1*. October 2012. http://www.singularityweblog.com/ray-kurzweil-on-singularity-1-on-1/3; accessed May 14, 2014.

"Be/Come the Cy/Borg." Kevin Warwick interviewed by Nikola Danaylov on *Singularity 1 on 1*. 2011. http://www.singularityweblog.com/?s=Kevin+Warwick; accessed June 2, 2014.

Do You Want to Live Forever? Channel 4 documentary. Producer and director Christopher Sykes. Windfall Film, 2006. http://www.youtube.com/watch?v=JtHgIJ6kalk; accessed May 14, 2014.

"Health, Longevity and Regenerative Medicine with Dr. Aubrey de Grey." Interviewed by Phil Micans. August 3, 2012. http://www.youtube.com/watch?v=sbC3_kOclxI; accessed May 14, 2014.

"Kevin Warwick—Implants & Technology: The Future of Healthcare?" TEDx Warwick, March 22, 2012. http://youtu.be/Z8HeFNJjujo; accessed June 2, 2014.

"Longevity Escape Velocity May Be Closer Than We Think." Aubrey de Grey interviewed by Nikola Danaylov on *Singularity 1 on 1*. 2011. http://www.singularityweblog.com/aubrey-de-greys-singularity-podcast-longevity-escape-velocity-maybe-closer-than-we-think/; accessed May 14, 2014.

"Max More Interview." Max More interviewed by Nikola Danaylov on *Singularity 1 on 1*. August 8, 2013. http://www.youtube.com/watch?v=JoxiX9mPB_s; accessed May 14, 2014.

"Natasha Vita-More." Natasha Vita-More interviewed by Nikola Danaylov on *Singularity 1 on 1*. 2011. http://www.singularityweblog.com/natasha-vita-more-on-singularity-1-on-1/; accessed June 2, 2014.

"Ordinary...Extraordinary: Life with a Bionic Arm." Nigel Ackland interviewed by Nikola Danaylov on *Singularity 1 on 1*. June 2013. http://www.singularityweblog.com/nigel-ackland-bionic-arm/; accessed June 3, 2014.

"Pursue the Big Challenges." David Ferrucci interviewed by Nikola Danaylov on *Singularity 1 on 1*. No date. http://www.singularityweblog.com/david-ferrucci-on-singularity-1-on-1-pursue-the-big-challenges/; accessed May 2, 2014.

"The End Is Not the End." Giulio Prisco interviewed by Nikola Danaylov on *Singularity 1 on 1*. 2013. http://www.singularityweblog.com/giulio-prisco-on-singularity-1-on-1/; accessed June 3, 2014.

Transcendent Man: The Life and Ideas of Ray Kurzweil. DVD. 86 min. Directed by Barry Ptolemy. Ptolemic Studios. 2009.

"Whole Body Prosthetic." Natasha Vita-More interviewed by Nikola Danaylov on *Singularity 1 on 1*. September 2013. https://www.youtube.com/watch?v=8LucitzhNQ8&feature=player_embedded; accessed June 3, 2014.

"You Have to Take Risks to Be Part of the Future." Kevin Warwick interviewed by Nikola Danaylov on *Singularity 1 on 1*. 2010. http://www.singularityweblog.com/kevin-warwick-on-singularity-podcast-you-have-to-take-risks-to-be-part-of-the-future/; accessed June 2, 2014.

INDEX

Other titles by David Herbert...

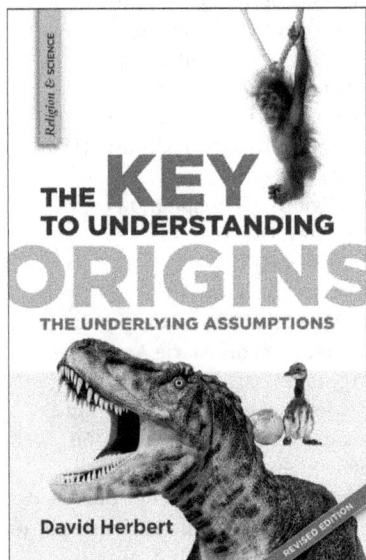

THE KEY TO UNDERSTANDING ORIGINS
The underlying assumptions

By David Herbert

BEGINNING WITH THE religious nature of man, Dr. Herbert shows how a belief in either naturalism or supernaturalism, determines what your position will be. He examines the basic tenets of each (and their variations) and opens the subject up for investigation and dialogue.

ISBN 978–1-894400-53–4

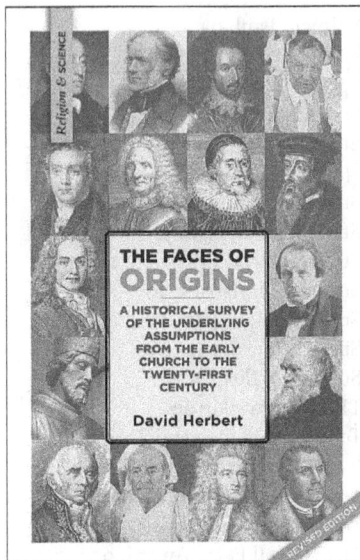

THE FACES OF ORIGINS
A historical survey of the underlying assumptions from the early church to the twenty-first century

By David Herbert

TRACING THE historical understanding of origins from the early church to the present, Herbert examines the philosophical presuppositions that existed behind Western worldviews. An enlightening read!

ISBN 978–1-894400-45-9

Visit us online at www.joshuapress.com

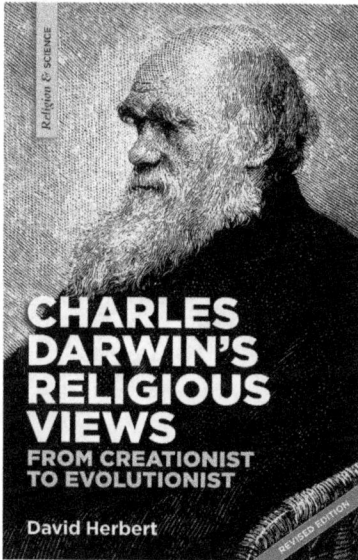

CHARLES DARWIN'S RELIGIOUS VIEWS

From creationist to evolutionist

By David Herbert

A SPIRITUAL BIOGRAPHY that focuses primarily on the religious experiences of Charles Darwin's life—demonstrating how Darwin's rejection of the Bible led him to adopt the naturalistic assumptions that were foundational to his belief in evolutionism.

ISBN 978–1-894400-30–5

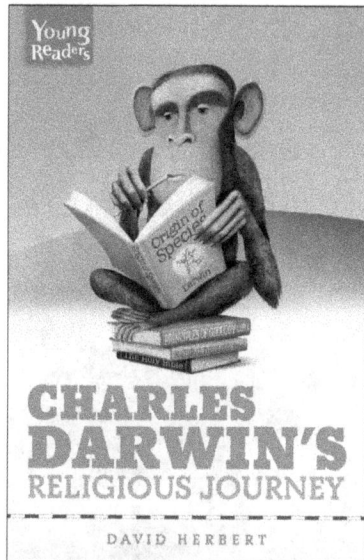

CHARLES DARWIN'S RELIGIOUS JOURNEY

By David Herbert

WRITTEN FOR YOUNG PEOPLE, this book traces Charles' life— from his voyage around the world on HMS *Beagle* to his research and experiments on his return to England. Complete with maps and photos.

ISBN 978–1-894400-34–3

COMPANION WORKBOOK
ISBN 978–1-894400-35–0

Other titles available from Joshua Press...

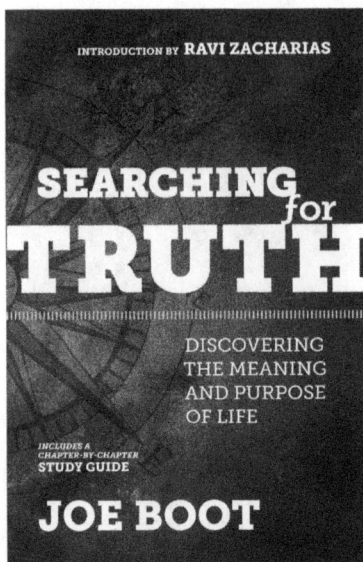

SEARCHING FOR TRUTH
Discovering the meaning
and purpose of life

By Joe Boot

BEGINNING WITH a basic understanding of the world, Joe Boot explains the biblical worldview, giving special attention to the life and claims of Jesus Christ. He wrestles with questions about suffering, truth, morality and guilt.

ISBN 978–1-894400-40-4

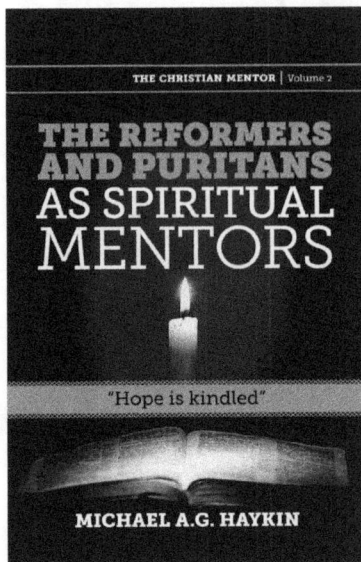

The Christian Mentor | Volume 2
THE REFORMERS AND PURITANS AS SPIRITUAL MENTORS
"Hope is kindled"

By Michael A. G. Haykin

REFORMERS SUCH as Tyndale, Cranmer and Calvin, and Puritans Richard Greenham, John Owen, etc. are examined to see how their display of the light of the gospel provides us with models of Christian conviction and living who can speak into our lives today.

ISBN 978–1-894400-39-8

Visit us online at www.joshuapress.com

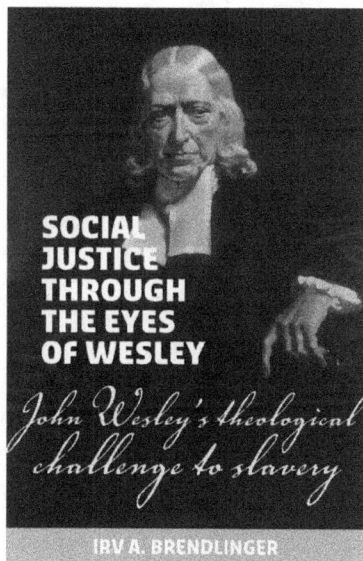

SOCIAL JUSTICE THROUGH THE EYES OF WESLEY

John Wesley's theological challenge to slavery

By Irv A. Brendlinger

THIS BOOK brings to light John Wesley's convictions about slavery and demonstrates how his theology compelled him to work to abolish it—writing, supporting and interacting with key players in the anti-slavery movement.

ISBN 978–1–894400-23–7

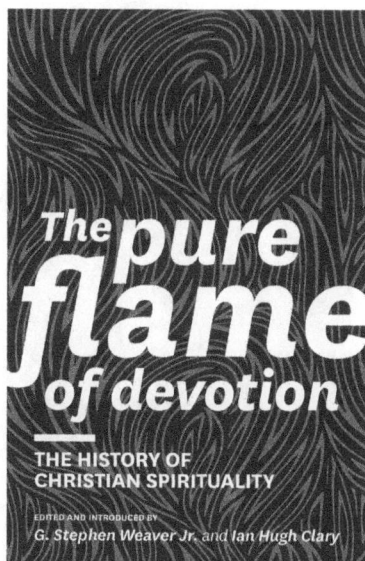

THE PURE FLAME OF DEVOTION

The history of Christian spirituality

Edited by G. Stephen Weaver Jr. and Ian Hugh Clary

THIS VOLUME is meant to ignite your interest and understanding of key time periods and pivotal people from various eras of church history. Each of the exceptional contributors skillfully expounds the vitality and richness of the spirituality of their subjects.

ISBN 978–1–894400-54–1 (PB)
ISBN 978–1–894400-55–8 (HC)

Deo Optimo et Maximo Gloria
To God, best and greatest, be glory

joshua press

www.joshuapress.com